ELEMENTS
OF
HOMILETIC

A Method for Preparing to Preach

O.C. Edwards, Jr.

ELEMENTS OF HOMILETIC

A Method for Preparing to Preach

PUEBLO PUBLISHING COMPANY

New York

Design: Frank Kacmarcik

Scriptural pericopes quoted from the Revised
Standard Version.

The author and publisher gratefully acknowledge
permission to reprint portions of the copyrighted
works listed in the Acknowledgments section.

ISBN: 0-916134-55-5

Printed in the United States of America

Contents

Foreword

This book is written to be a companion volume to *Elements of Rite* by Aidan Kavanagh O.S.B. which, in turn, was inspired by that marvelous vade mecum of all who try to hang English sentences together in lucid prose, *The Elements of Style* by William Strunk, Jr. and E.B. White. Differences between the subjects treated necessitate differences in the format of the three books. Strunk and White, in giving instruction on writing English prose well, were able to state their rules in the imperative and to illustrate good and bad usage in the explanatory paragraphs that followed the rules. Kavanagh, while also enunciating canons of usage, was concerned with how actions were to be carried out well. Thus he could describe a poor performance, but his description was not itself a performance as the bad sentences of Strunk and White were. His examples are less numerous, therefore; he uses the indicative to imply the imperative, and his exhortations are explicitly grounded in liturgical theology. This book is not so much concerned with canons of usage as it is in delineating a methodical procedure. It is about how-to-do-it-at-all rather than how-to-do-it-artfully. It, therefore, uses the imperative to give step-by-step instructions and thus belongs more to the genre of instructions on how to uncrate and assemble a bicycle than it does to that which inculcates connoisseurship.

Even so elementary a task could not be performed without the assistance of many people. My first debt of gratitude is to Fr. Kavanagh, who nominated me for the job of writing this book, and my second is to our publisher, Bernard Benziger, who has encouraged and assisted me in many ways. A third debt of gratitude goes to Fred Baumer C.PP.S., whom I found practically on my doorstep with the wide knowledge of the homilist's art that is revealed in his cassette course, *Preacher: Storyteller of God*. I have also borrowed freely from a number of other writers in the field, generally without acknowledgment at the point of borrowing, though they are all listed in the appendix on Resources. My basic thought on the subject still bears the imprint of my first teacher in preaching thirty years ago, that canny Scot, The Rev. Dr. James T. Cleland. Biblical quotations, unless otherwise indicated, are from the Revised Standard Version.

In this volume, as in all my writing and thinking, my deepest debt is to the conversation of the friend to whose memory this work is dedicated, The Very Rev. Urban T. Holmes, III. His wisdom on the subject of preaching is indicated in these words from a book that came out at the time of his death: "The sermon or homily . . . has as its object the inscape of existence, not the landscape. Preaching is not teaching. As an act of evangelizing the deep memory, it needs to reveal to us the inner person, not describe the externals" (*Turning to Christ*, p. 216).

R.I.P.

Urban T. Holmes, III

1930-81

Tell it not in Gath, publish it not in the
streets of Ashkelon.

2 Sam. 1:20

I. Toward a Definition

One of the most obvious trends in contemporary Church life is a confluence of Christendom. While many differences remain between the major branches of Christianity, there is nevertheless a discernible centripetal movement. One of the most obvious manifestations of that coming together is in worship. A quarter of a century ago Sunday duty for the average Catholic meant going to a Mass at which the liturgy of the Word passed unobtrusively while for a mainline American Protestant it meant attending a service at which a half-hour long sermon was preached and the hymns, prayers, and readings that preceded it were regarded as and often referred to as the "preliminaries." Now Catholics devote much attention to the proclamation of the Word of God, both in the vernacular reading of the proper lections from scripture and in the homily that follows. Protestants, on the other hand, now have a far more liturgical and often eucharistic context for their preaching than they had formerly and have begun to adopt the Church calendar, the three-year lectionary cycle, vestments, fixed liturgies rather than extempore prayers, and many other features that had been previously identified with Catholic worship.

While the ultimate explanation for this confluence is probably theological and intermediate reasons are sociological, the most obvious proximate historical cause of the major shift in Catholic ethos is the Second Vatican Council. Its *Constitution on the Sacred Liturgy* especially is quite explicit about the importance of the proclamation of the Word of God. It speaks of "the two parts which, in a certain sense, go to make up the Mass, namely, the liturgy of the word and the eucharistic liturgy" and goes on to say that these two parts are "so closely connected with each other that they form but a single act of worship" (#56). Indeed, the homily "is to be highly esteemed as part of the liturgy itself; in fact, at those Masses which are celebrated with the assistance of the people on Sundays and feasts of obligation, it should not be omitted except for a serious reason" (#52).

The content of sermons is also specified:

The sermon, moreover, should draw its content mainly from scripture and liturgical sources, and its character should be that of a proclamation of God's wonderful works in the history of salvation, the mystery of Christ, ever made present and active in us, especially in the celebration of the liturgy. (#35).

This new emphasis on preaching, however, has caught many deacons, presbyters, and even bishops in a state of unpreparedness. It is all very well to say that one should preach, but what does one do when one preaches? Many have felt like Noah in the comedy routine of Bill Cosby. When God said, "Noah, build me an ark," Noah replied: "Ri-i-ight! What's an ark?" This lack of basic understanding of the task of preaching was brought home to me in one of the preparations I made to write this book. In order to investigate the present state of preaching in the Catholic Church I began to go every Sunday I was free to a different parish to hear what was being proclaimed and how the proclamation was made. Here are some of the results:

• On the Sunday beginning the Week of Prayer for Christian Unity I heard a homily that was more an instruction on the current state of ecumenical negotiations than anything else. This lecture, given in a flat, unemotional voice, listed positive accomplishments: we no longer re-baptize, there is better cooperation on weddings, etc, but there is no inter-communion yet. The speaker seemed in favor of Christian unity and appeared to regret that more has not yet been achieved, but his approach was legal—informing the faithful of exactly what is and is not allowed. Only at the end did he refer to the scriptural propers, although his allusion was appropriate. And his only emotional appeal also came at the very end when he said that we should feel about the disunity of Christians as we would feel if we sat down at the family table and there were empty seats.

• On the Fourth Sunday in Lent I heard an Irish Jesuit give what amounted to an Ignatian meditation on the gospel, John 9:1-13, 24-38, delivered with a delightful brogue. He began by reconstructing imaginatively the story of the healing of the man born blind and then went on to apply it to the life of the faithful by saying (with, it seemed to me, little basis in the text) that the sin of the Pharisees and chief priests was envy. He then defined envy and illustrated it in the lives of children, and showed how it

3

is present in all states of life, including that of priests. After saying that we should learn to recognize it and its cause in ourselves and noting the theological objection to it that it denies the presence of Christ in the uniqueness of the envied person, he said that when we overcome envy we become like the blind man who was healed.

• On the Fourth Sunday in Easter the sermon I heard, after a tip of the hat to Mother's Day, concerned and was addressed to children who were making their first communion. In a vocabulary and with concepts that were appropriate to this audience the preacher alluded to the gospel by saying that just as the Good Shepherd calls his sheep by name, so they would be called by name when they received holy communion that day. The parents were then told that, just as one may enter the sheepfold by the gate or by some other way, so life is like a wall in which there are four doors: wealth, power, fame, Jesus (surely the options are more numerous!). The importance of parental example was stressed.

• On the World Day of Prayer for Vocations I heard a young priest begin his homily by reading a letter from the Cardinal on the subject of vocations. Then he told of going out to his seminary for ordinations on the eleventh anniversary of his own admission to the presbyterate. After telling about an interruption of the event by women seeking ordination, he told of the critical annual decline in the size of seminary classes. Next he spoke of vocations to the priesthood, to the religious life, and to the lay state. In the course of the homily he made some apt references to scripture. As a coda he spoke also of the "ministry of forgiveness," since the ordination Mass he had attended had been on the day the Pope was shot and the Holy Father's forgiveness of his assassin had been made known.

• The specially made altar frontal was decorated with a mortar board over a rolled diploma in one corner and a lamp of learning diagonally across from it with a legend in between of "God's Blessing . . . Graduates." The Trinity Sunday homily was about having a personal relation with each of the divine Persons and there was an extended analogy to the family. Rain on the roof, a wailing siren, and the soft, Spanish-accented voice of the preacher combined to make hearing difficult. It was acknowledged that how God can be both three and one is a mystery to be accepted on faith. Other than the analogy to family life, there were virtually no illustrations and few allusions to the Bible.

One could not easily derive a definition of Christian preaching from these examples. There were a number of special days with no liturgical status to which attention was called from the pulpit, one heard Church regulations and moral exhortations, and there was even an effort at theological analysis. The homilies, though, had little in common that enabled the listener to induct what one does when one preaches. The nearest to a definition afforded by those examples would be something like: "talks given at Mass." Since in order to do something well, one must know what one is attempting to do, an effort will be made to define preaching. At first the definition will not be normative but phenomenological. That is, it will not so much say what preaching ought to be as offer a description broad enough to cover almost everything that takes place in Christian preaching. This description will be taken as a definition of "sermon" and will not be limited to what Catholics do, but will seek to include all Christian preaching. It will be followed by an effort to refine and restrict the definition so that it will apply to the homilies expected at Mass by the *Constitution on the Sacred Liturgy*. Thus this second definition will be specifically Catholic and will take on a normative dimension.

It should be pointed out at the beginning, though, that there is no significant difference in meaning between the English words *sermon* and *homily*. The decision indicated above to distinguish between them is purely arbitrary and for the sake of convenience; it has no basis in the general history of the usage of the two words. It may be, though, that the fathers of the Second Vatican Council used the word "homily" more consistently for preaching at the eucharistic assembly because "sermon" had a pre-conciliar association with long, didactic, sometimes apologetic addresses that could be made on any occasion. By using homily they hoped to avoid evoking such connotations.

Some scholars have tried to break down the etymology of homily into its original Greek components and thus suggested that it means "communicating with a crowd," but surely this is the etymological fallacy of assuming that the present meaning of a word is governed by the roots from which it was derived. The word *homilia* existed in Greek and was used in essentially the meaning of its English cognate for many centuries, just as *sermo* had a similar place in Latin. Grady Davis sums up the evidence very well when he says that as a rhetorical term in secular Greek *homilia* meant an informal, discursive talk characterized by digressions, but in its technical Christian meaning it came soon to refer to an ordered exposition of a passage in scripture (*Design for Preaching*, p. 162). The *Constitution on the Sacred Liturgy* uses sermon and homily interchangeably. Thus the words are synonymous and the following distinction between them is offered only for the purpose of analysis.

A definition of sermon that encompasses most of the phenomena that bear that label is:

A sermon is a speech delivered in a Christian assembly for worship by an authorized person that applies some point of doctrine, usually drawn from a biblical passage, to the lives of the members of the congregation with the purpose of moving them by the use of narrative analogy and other rhetorical devices to accept that application and to act on the basis of it.

Every element in this definition is important. To say that a sermon is a speech is to communicate information devoid of surprise, but much that will be said later in the book derives from the difference between oral and written discourse. Public speaking is a particular sort of transaction between a speaker and an audience. One who wishes to communicate effectively through this medium will pay heed to the principles that have been discovered to operate on such occasions.

There is more surprise in saying that a sermon is delivered in a Christian assembly for worship. After all, the most basic Christian proclamation is evangelization, is seeking to communicate the good news of salvation in Jesus Christ to those who have not yet heard this message in such a way that they could respond to it. Now that going to church is no longer required for respectability in this country, one seldom finds the totally unconverted in Christian assemblies. Thus a sermon is distinguished from evangelization. This is not to say that one is more important than the other, but only to note that they are not the same thing. Christian preaching is also to be distinguished from catechesis, from Christian teaching.

Yet both the proclamation of the gospel and instruction in the faith occur in sermons delivered at worship. Not all of the faithful assembled on Sunday morning are equally faithful in the sense that they believe the Christian construction of reality with the same degree of conviction and commitment. Fr. Fred Baumer has distinguished between the worshiping assembly and the worshiping community, i.e., all of those who are present when worship occurs and those who are really bound together in faith. The congregation on Sunday morning will be as mixed a bag as the audience of Peter the Hermit T.S. Eliot described in one of the Choruses from his play, *The Rock*:

And among his hearers were a few good men,
Many who were evil,
And most who were neither,
Like all men in all places.

Some of those at Mass will be in need of conversion, some will need their faith reinforced, and most who live in our very secular society will find the Catholic faith in continuous need of relegitimation. Participating in worship and listening to sermons is a vital part of the total effort to construct reality in a Christian way. There are, of course, many other purposes for preaching in the Christian assembly, but the others will be discussed later.

Preaching is not done by just anyone. All Christian bodies have ways of authorizing spokespersons and only the utterances of members of that group carry the authority of preaching. This authorization has a number of aspects. It implies that the speaker has been lifted up by the community to represent God to it and it to God. A recognition of gifts and calling is involved as well as a certification of training and commissioning. All of these things are necessary to give the speech of a Christian the authority of preaching. Naturally, there are other members of the body who speak. Occasionally there is one with a charism of a prophet who will communicate with the Church and society from outside the official structures and channels. Charisms, however, are bestowed directly by God, and the Spirit blows where it wishes. The preacher of sermons, though, is representative of the community and receives divine authorization through the community.

Just as preaching is not done by everyone, it is also not all speech in the Christian assembly by authorized persons. It is a particular genre of speech in which the historic faith is brought to bear on the lives of the community. Sermons are concerned with the "So What?" of Christian belief. They deal with living out the faith that was professed in baptism.

Because this first definition is phenomenological rather than normative, it cannot specify that all sermons are based on portions of holy scripture. Once during the Second Vatican Council a Benedictine theologian was visiting the campus of the liberal arts college where I taught. When he heard that the local Methodist minister was to be the speaker in chapel that day, he was delighted because he looked forward to hearing some real biblical preaching. As it turned out, there was not a single reference to holy writ in the entire talk. Since the argument from *esse* to *posse* is good, one is able to have a sermon that does not seek to focus the perspective of a biblical passage on contemporary Christian living and celebration. The sad impoverished possibility is borne out by some of the preaching I heard when I went sermon tasting in Roman Catholic parishes in preparation for writing this book. This is simply to say that there can be bad sermons. To march under the banner of sermons, though, a speech must seek to apply a point of doctrine to the lives of members of the congregation.

The attentive reader may have recognized by now that the exercise under way is form criticism. It is an effort to list the discriminating characteristics of a literary genre or *Gattung*. Saying that this genre accomplishes its purpose through the use of narrative analogy and other rhetorical devices calls attention to a marked feature of the sermon. It is a form of persuasion rather than demonstration. While deficiency in logic is a serious shortcoming in a sermon, the major means used to convince the audience are not airtight arguments. Rather, the preacher seeks to persuade by analogies and examples. Usually these are narrative. Part of the explanation for this strategy comes from the oral nature of homiletical communication; it is keyed to the ear instead of the eye. Another part comes from the way that the Bible does most of its proclamation through narration. Still another part is derived from something to be discussed in more detail later, the way that the sermon is directed more to the "deep memory" of archetypal images than it is to the surface memory of conceptual thought. Many preachers never seem to learn the difference between a sermon and a lecture. The difference lies mainly in the strategy for persuasion that is employed, the nature of the argument and the evidence that is offered.

This point cannot be made too strongly. Since emphasis on the proclamation of the word has come to the Roman Catholic Church very recently and since most clergy seldom have or take the opportunity to hear someone else preach, one of the major reasons for a low standard of preaching is the lack of good examples. While there are Catholic preachers around fully as good as the best Protestant "pulpit giants," others who preach seldom get a chance to hear them.

There is a lack of good models. Most Protestant ministers spent most of the Sundays before they went to seminary attending divine service in which a sermon was considered to be the major ingredient. By the time they began to preach themselves, they knew what good preaching sounded like. Few Catholics have had that sort of exposure. The narrative shape of preaching, then, is something that they have had to intuit.

The last element in this definition of a sermon is that it seeks to move members of the congregation to accept the application of the point of doctrine to their lives made in the sermon and to act on the basis of it. Several important points are involved here. First, preaching seeks to *move* people. This is to say that there is to be emotional as well as intellectual appeal. The use of narrative assists greatly in that effort. In the history of preaching there has been, of course, sheer emotionalism that has cultivated hysteria. Such tactics are manipulative and immoral. Yet human beings are not computers. A person is not converted who has come only to accept that the Christian construction of reality is intellectually valid. No, full conversion requires that one's life be centered around that conviction. While some emotional responses are shallow, the deepest responses always have a powerful emotional dynamic. It is this dynamic that leads the convert to act on the basis of a newfound conviction. Congregations, then, are to be *moved* and they are to be moved to *act*. Beliefs that do not have behavioral implications and impetus are not significantly different from unbelief.

The narrowing of this general definition of sermon to the point that it is normative for Catholic homilies looks like this:

A homily is a sermon preached at the eucharistic assembly by a bishop, presbyter, or deacon that applies a point of doctrine drawn from that day's gospel to the lives of the members of the congregation with the purpose of moving them by the use of narrative analogy and other rhetorical devices to accept that application and to act on the basis of it both in their participation in the liturgy and as they go forth into the world.

It should be obvious that homily is a species of the genus sermon. The significance of the restrictions in this definition can be appreciated readily. A homily is a sermon preached at Mass. The liturgy of the word and the eucharistic liturgy go together. Christians are "constituted" by the eucharist, as the fourth-century martyr Felix said at his trial (quoted by Massey H. Shepherd, *The Worship of the Church*, p. 5).

The persons authorized to preach are bishops, presbyters, and deacons. To say this is merely to note what is set down in The Code of Canon Law of the Roman Church: the faculty to preach eucharistic homilies may be granted only to bishops, priests, and deacons (C. 1342). In recent years there has been a certain amount of interest in having lay persons, especially members of religious communities, preach at Mass. Someone has suggested that lay Dominicans are authorized to preach by virtue of membership in the Order of Preachers, but Simon Tugwell O.P. has argued convincingly to the contrary (*The Way of the Preacher*, pp. 132-33). This restriction also appears to be supported by the *Constitution on the Sacred Liturgy* when it says: "In liturgical celebrations each person, minister or layperson, who has an office to perform, should do all of, but only, those parts which pertain to his office by the nature of the rite and the principles of liturgy" (#28). In the guidelines concerning the homily at Mass promulgated by the Archdiocese of New York there is provision for laity to make remarks at points in the liturgy other than that specified for the homily. More inclusive provisions may lie in the future, however, since many recognize that the ability to preach is at least a talent and may be a gift or charism. At any rate, all persons do not share in it equally and the insistence on ordained status may mean that the faithful are subjected to bad preaching when good is available.

An arbitrary and editorial note is injected in the specification that the homily always be based on the gospel. The *Constitution on the Liturgy* does say that "the sermon should draw its content mainly from scriptural and liturgical sources" and goes on to say that "its character should be that of a proclamation of God's wonderful works in the history of salavation, the mystery of Christ," which seems likely to be the part to be derived from the Bible, and that this is "ever made present and active within us, especially in the celebration of the liturgy" (#35), which is obviously to draw on liturgical sources. It also says that it is "from the scripture that lessons are read and explained in the homily" (#24), which sounds like an invalidation of all those homilies I heard that did not explain the lessons appointed for that day. Some, however, would say that the homily should treat all of the lessons appointed, not just the gospel. According to Skudlarek, there are many who believe that doing so is involved in the very concept of liturgical preaching (*The Word in Worship*, p. 40). Since he himself has pointed out that epistles and gospels are given course readings rather than chosen for their common themes in the three-year lectionary cycle, and since it is so hard to make one point clearly in the time available for a homily, I believe that the homily should begin with the gospel and bring in the other lessons only if they are serendipitous. I am comforted to have the support of my colleague Fr. Kavanagh in this. His nineteenth principle is: "The homily is always on the gospel of the day, and one never preaches unless one has something to say." He also takes the position that the preacher is the president of the assembly.

The final way in which the definition of sermon is sharpened to refer to the homily at Mass is that the action in response to it has two aspects. First, it enables the worshipers to participate more fully in the eucharistic liturgy because they have been fully involved in the liturgy of the word. The history of salvation and the mystery of Christ that are proclaimed in the homily are made available and experienced in the sacrament. The appropriation of this salvation is made more self-conscious by the preaching that has preceded it. That salvation, however, is not confined in its present expression to the duration of the assembly. It is to be lived out in the daily life of all who share in it. They receive suggestions of how this is done appropriately in the homily.

So much for defining what one does when one preaches. Now it is time to see how it is done.

II. Interpreting The Gospel

1. *Begin by asking yourself what your motive for preaching is and what model of a preacher is in your mind.*

It is much easier to do something if you know in advance what you want to do, if you have some idea of what it looks like when someone does that thing. This applies to preaching as well as to any other activity. One seldom accomplishes great things accidentally. To preach effectively, then, you must begin by asking what effective preaching is, what its objective is, who does it well, and what makes their efforts so successful.

Motives are always mixed, of course. Some of your less noble motives might be that the pastor told you to and you do not want to make him mad, or that you want your parishioners to think you eloquent, holy, witty, or profound. It is unlikely that anyone outgrows such inclinations in this life.

There are other motives that are nobler, but which still miss what preaching is basically about. One such motive is to inform the faithful. Certainly people do acquire information from sermons, but the impartation of it is a by-product of preaching. Another motive might be to encourage members of the congregation to obey the laws of the church. Like Cato the Elder who is supposed to have ended every speech by saying, "Carthage must be destroyed," a priest of whom I have heard closed even his Christmas and Easter sermons by urging parents to have their babies baptized within the canonical time. Canons, rubrics, and other forms of church regulations are important, but they are not properly the subject of the homily. St. Paul, in fact, went to some lengths to distinguish between gospel and law.

And the gospel is what preaching is about. In Greek, the verb we translate "to preach" is *kēryssein*, which is related to the noun *kēryx*, "a herald." Modern New Testament scholars often use the noun for the message of a herald, *kērygma*, as a synonym for gospel. As the popular musical of the same name has made known, the derivation of our English word "gospel" is "god spell," an Old English expression meaning "good tidings" or "good news." Thus it translates exactly the Greek *euangelion* and has been used in that sense from the tenth century. (A popular theory that "god spell" means "a story about a god," however attractive, has been refuted in the *Oxford English Dictionary*.) To preach, then, is to proclaim the good news that in Jesus God has acted finally and decisively for the reclamation of a lost world.

The motive for preaching can be expressed in the vocabulary of liturgical theology as assisting the people of God to celebrate the mystery of Christ. Because Jesus died and rose again we can be grafted into his body through baptism and share in the paschal mys-

18

tery when we gather to make eucharist. Homilies based on the gospel for the day enable the faithful to participate more fully in the aspect of the total mystery of Christ that is being celebrated that day and to live out its implications. But more of that later.

Another way of describing the motive for preaching is in the vocabulary of the sociology of knowledge: preaching is done to help people to construct reality in a Christian way. In our society anyone who believes the Catholic faith is swimming against the current. As Peter Berger has pointed out, the "knowledge industry"—the media and the schools—presents to the nation a view of life in which Christianity is irrelevant. Those who are to be maintained in their faith must have continual reinforcement of it by the support of the persons who are most important in their lives, their "probability structure," as the sociologists call it. Preaching and the liturgy make it possible for people to acquire faith and to hold on to it after they get it. A homily that does not have the inculcation and maintenance of a Christian construction of reality as one of its major purposes is inadequately motivated.

Closely related to your motive for preaching is the model of the ideal preacher that you hold in your mind. There is an old chestnut to the effect that "I don't know much about art, but I know what I like." This is to say that our criteria are often unconscious rather than conscious, implicit rather than explicit. Yet it is possible to start with what you like— whether in preaching or another art form—and ask yourself what you like about it. This makes the implicit criteria explicit. Since it is inevitable that we pattern our own participation in an activity on that of those we think do it best, one of the reasons to identify our models is that we may discover we have chosen the wrong ones. What they do when they preach may be something less than proclaiming the gospel. And if we have been imitating them in our preaching, we will have been going about it wrong.

If, however, we discover that our models have been good, we can then ask what makes them good. If we are to do what they do, how do we go about it? What steps will we take? Keeping all of this in mind when we sit down to begin our preparation of a homily will insure that what we end up with really is a homily.

2. *Commence the preparation for next Sunday's homily not later than Monday.*

As a homilist who takes the Word of God seriously and the people of God seriously, you can hardly do less. Think of the number of persons who will hear you preach. In a good sized parish that will be several hundred to a thousand or more. Multiply their number by the time you will preach, say ten to twenty minutes. Then divide that number by sixty and you will have the number of human hours that go into listening to you. Your effort in preparation should be in proportion to theirs in listening. Few will be able to realize the goal of great Protestant preachers of the past who felt that they had to spend an hour in preparation for every minute in the pulpit. Still, no one can preach well without preparing well.

There are those blessed or cursed with a glib tongue who can speak entertainingly with very little advance thought. I say "or cursed" because for them there must be a great temptation to get by with "winging it." Yet their people deserve their best thought, not any old thing they can come up with on the spur of the moment. And certainly those who lack the gift need to do what they can to make up for the lack by the care of their preparation. Often they want to excuse themselves by saying, "There's no point in trying because I'm going to bomb anyway." They have the wrong end of the stick on that argument: to retrieve the situation at all, they must spend more and not less time in getting ready to preach than those who have a natural talent for it.

It takes time to get ready to preach. Anyone using the method of preparation outlined in this book will not be able to think up something for Sunday's homily while sitting in the confessional on Saturday afternoon. There are two things that take time. The first is study: exegesis of the gospel and boning up on the situation to which it is to be applied. The second is thought. There has to be a lot of mulling over the fruits of your exegesis before you know where it should be brought to bear on the lives of your parishioners that Sunday. More will be said of this later. For the moment, though, plan to begin on Monday and put in some time every day until Sunday. (The method of preparation detailed in this book is for homilies for Sundays or major feasts since few priests can spend the time required more than once a week.)

3. *Initiate your preparation with prayer and continue to pray at each stage of preparation.*

To begin with, there is no point in preaching if you do not believe in praying. Preaching grows out of the conviction that life is about God, the God who was revealed in Jesus Christ and who is worshiped in the church. God's ordained servants who serve him in the church and who lead his people in worship need to be persons of prayer themselves. And one of the things that all Christians should pray about is their work. While all of life should be an offering to God, the work one does is a matter of vocation, a matter of the particular task for which one was created and called.

Furthermore, we should want our preaching to succeed, to be effective in accomplishing its purpose. Undoubtedly God is trying at all times to get through to us and to direct us into the way that we should go, but often our preoccupations act like static "jamming" his message. We need to be in tune with him, then, we need to be open to hearing his voice.

All of this need not be too mystical. The only impression we have may be that our mind seems to be functioning with abnormal efficiency that day. Yet any experienced preacher knows what it is like to get an idea. It usually comes suddenly and unexpectedly, but there is a vivid impression that this is it, that we have struck pay dirt. Poets can talk about inspiration without any particular theology to back it up. Why should the church's presbyters feel embarrassed by the idea that the God to whose service they have devoted their lives may wish to use them occasionally as one of the channels through which he speaks to his people? (There is, however, an equal if not greater danger in the opposite direction of confusing our will and word with the word and will of God.)

Part of the mystery of preaching is that much of what it accomplishes was never envisioned by the preacher. Anyone who has preached often has had experiences of discovering that what was said in a homily had peculiar appropriateness for someone in the congregation whose presence or need had not been anticipated. And the way that people hear things is often not what one intended to convey, but for them it is more important than what was intended. Such "coincidences" happen more often with those who consider prayer to be an important part of their preparation for preaching.

Such prayer should not be confined to the beginning of the process, like the old custom of writing *J.M.J.* at the top of a page. Much of the working out of a sermon is an interior dialogue. In such a dialogue you can address God as easily as yourself. Doing so will change remarkably your attitude toward what you are doing.

Finally, the prayer should continue to the time of delivery. The prophet Isaiah told us:

For as the rain and the snow come
down from heaven,
and return not thither but water
the earth,
making it bring forth and sprout,
giving seed to the sower and bread
to the eater,
so shall my word be that goes forth
from my mouth;
it shall not return to me empty,
but it shall accomplish that which I
purpose,
and prosper in the thing for which
I sent it (55:10, 11).

Our prayer in the pulpit can be that God's word spoken through us will not return empty, but accomplish its purpose and prosper in doing what God intended it to.

4. *Read the gospel with the expectation that God will speak to you through it and that he will speak to his people through your preaching.*

Preaching presupposes not only a belief in prayer but also a belief in scripture and a belief in the task of preaching itself. The belief in scripture is not just a general intellectual assent to propositions about what the Bible is supposed to do, but is an affective conviction that that actually happens. The Bible tells us not only the basic gospel message of what God has done for us in Christ, it also tells us God's perspective on the events of our lives. This perspective is seldom found by looking up the right prooftext; the process is far more complex than that. Yet it is from the Bible that we come to understand what issues are at stake in the events of our lives. It may be hard for us to believe that until we have had some experience of having our own lives illuminated by a passage we were reading, as a dark path at night is revealed in a sudden flash of lightning. Those under obligation to recite the office have frequently had such experience while reading the Psalms. If it can work for us, it can work for others.

It is this knowledge that contemporary experience can be understood from perspectives acquired in Bible reading that gives integrity to the whole enterprise of preaching. Otherwise we would be in the position of Old Mother Hubbard promising to give her poor dog a bone when she knew perfectly well that her cupboard was bare. The promises of Matthew 7:7, 8 apply to the preacher as well as to anyone else: "Ask, and it will be given you; seek, and you will find; knock, and it will be opened to you. For every one who asks receives, and he who seeks finds, and to him who knocks it will be opened." When we sit down to read the lections for the Sunday we are to preach, we should do so with the expectation that they will have something to say that our people need to hear. We should approach this reading with the same sense of anticipation that something is going to happen that the person has who always carries an umbrella when praying for rain.

There is, of course, an alternative approach which is to be avoided. That is to approach the lections with the anticipation that something can be found there that can be bent to one's own purposes.

'When I use a word,' Humpty Dumpty said in a rather scornful tone, 'it means just what I choose it to mean—neither more nor less.'

'The question is,' said Alice, 'whether you can make words mean so many different things.'

'The question is,' said Humpty Dumpty, 'which is to be master—that's all.'

When the word at stake is God's Word, let us hope that we will never master it in the sense of overpowering it. In responding to the claim of Rudolf Bultmann that one has to approach the biblical text with a pre-understanding, Ernst Fuchs pointed out that it is not just a matter of our interpreting the text: the text also interprets us. It should therefore be approached with modesty as well as expectation.

5. *Read the gospel very carefully.*
Sometimes the obvious is the easiest thing to overlook. A lot of time can be saved later if you get off on the right foot. It is easy to glance over the lectionary hastily and gain an impression of what is being said, only to discover later that you had missed the point. When you discover that, you have to start all over.

The careful reading is not as easy as it sounds because most clergy try to get by with reading only one translation. When you do that, it is possible to think that an accident of English phrasing represents a significant aspect of the text. The only way to be sure that the text really says what you think it does is to test the translation. It is here that those who have studied Greek are most fortunate. No document in one language is ever translated into another language perfectly so that the exact thought with all its nuances and with no extraneous suggestions appears in the new language. There is a maxim to the effect that every translation is an interpretation. This is to say, among other things, that all translations resolve ambiguities that are left open in the original. Thus they close off possibilities for the reader to consider. The one who knows Greek knows the kinds of thoughts that can be expressed easily in that language and also knows interpretations that would seem unnatural. Another way of saying that is that knowledge of Greek protects you from anachronistic interpretation.

Since, however, most seminary graduates today have not studied the biblical languages, a way must be found to make do. One of these is to read the passage in several translations. Certainly that should be done for the verse on which your sermon idea turns, because it may not mean what you think it means. The Revised Standard Version is the well-known modern English translation which best reflects the structure of the Greek that lies behind it. This is not to say that other translations are less "accurate," but is rather to recognize that there are two schools of translators.

One seeks to give the best word-for-word rendering of the original and the other seeks to give the most adequate expression of the thought of the original in an idiomatic form of the language into which it is translated. The RSV translators and Lattimore in his *The Four Gospels and the Revelation* belong to the first school.

If you know other modern languages or Latin—or indeed any other ancient languages—these can offer fresh insight into the meaning of a passage.

6. Note any striking, unexpected narrative details, paying special attention to what is most difficult to understand or accept.

After thirty years of sitting down each week to study the Sunday gospel, I am continually amazed at how I continually see things that I had overlooked before. Such discoveries are often made in this first careful reading that we are talking about. There can be many reasons why the particular point had not been noticed previously. One is our unconscious tendency to harmonize the gospels, to approximate the way that something is said in one gospel to the way that it is said to another. At any rate, these discoveries are serendipitous indeed for the preacher because they often give you a germ of the idea for your sermon.

This point has been made particularly well by William Skudlarek, OSB:

As you ruminate on these texts, you will very likely find that there is a word or verse or passage that is especially troublesome. The reasons for this may be that you simply do not understand what the author is getting at. On the other hand, you may understand it all too well! Or it may be that the word sounds totally irrelevant or even offensive when placed vis-à-vis the particular people and the specific situations you have to deal with. The temptation, of course, will be to skip over these passages, to look for something that seems more appropriate, more suited to the situation at hand. But don't do it! Stay with the difficult passage. Wrestle with it, not letting it go until it gives you an answer (*The Word in Worship*, p. 54)

This good advice takes us farther along the process of sermon preparation than this stage of first familiarization with the passage to be preached from, but it will be worth remembering.

7. *Observe how God is depicted as moving in the lives of his people.*

We are still at a very early stage of sermon preparation, that of our preliminary reading of Sunday's gospel. The purpose of this step is to make certain that from the beginning we are aware of the crucial issue: the proclamation that is being made in this passage about how God is involved and working in the lives of his people. The question to ask is: what is God accomplishing here? It presupposes that he acts in comparable ways in the lives of people today; indeed, the gospel to be proclaimed is that he does so. Much work will have to be done on this later, but the important thing at this stage is to note it. Doing so will keep you on track.

8. *Examine manuscript variations to see what difference the alternatives make and which is more likely to be original.*

The discipline involved here is textual criticism, the effort to reconstruct exactly what words the sacred author wrote and in what order. This job is made necessary by the fact that for the first 1,400 years that the books of the New Testament existed each new volume had to be laboriously copied by hand. As in all handwork, minute variations were inevitable. Many variant readings were introduced into the text. The question to be asked today is: Which of those readings is what the original author actually wrote?

Textual criticism is a highly technical discipline and the average preacher of Sunday homilies will not be equipped to do it scientifically. There are, however, two reasons for including it as a step in sermon preparation. The first is that proclamation grows out of exegesis and we need to know what is involved in the scholar's interpretation of a passage, even if we cannot replicate all of the steps in that interpretive process. Secondly, and more practically, there are ways in which one who is not a trained scripture scholar can become aware of at least some of the major manuscript variations and involve them in his or her* efforts to understand the Sunday gospel.

---

*While it is expected that most of the users of this book will be Roman Catholics and the canon law does not at this time permit the ordination of women to the presbyterate or diaconate, it is hoped that it

Most modern translations, for instance, have marginal references to textual variations. I opened my RSV at random to a page on which is printed Luke 5:29-6:13a. There are three footnotes there. The first informs the reader that, while the translation of 5:29 refers to people "sitting" at a table, the Greek actually says "reclining," in accordance with the dining customs of the time. The next says that in some manuscripts 5:39 says that the old wine is "better" rather than "good." The third makes 6:1 date the walk through the grainfields on "the second sabbath after the first" rather than just on "a sabbath." Only the last two of these have to do with manuscript variation, since the first is a matter of translation. These two are fairly easy ones for finding the original reading. A basic principle of textual criticism is: That reading is to be preferred which best accounts for the others. In 5:39 a comparative seems called for and so the likelihood is that the original lacked it and the correction supplied it. In 6:1 it sounds like some copyist was dissatisfied with the vagueness of "a sabbath" and introduced the greater precision of "on the second sabbath after the first." These particular variants make little difference in the meaning of the passage, but enough do to make them always worth checking on. Examples of variants that make a big

will be used by clergy of other communions in which such ordination is permitted. Besides, the time may come when female Roman Catholics will have a need for such a book. For these reasons there is an effort to make the language referring to preachers sexually inclusive.

difference are: (a) Mark ends with 16:8 rather than 16:20 in the oldest manuscripts, (b) the story of the woman taken in adultery does not appear in the oldest manuscripts of John at 7:53-8:11 or anywhere else, and (c) the explicit trinitarian references that appears in the Vulgate of 1 John 5:7-8 appears in only four very late Greek manuscripts.

Commentaries also discuss the more important textual variations. For those who know Greek an excellent tool is Bruce M. Metzger, *A Textual Commentary on the Greek New Testament*, which gives the reasoning behind the readings and estimates of their probability in the *United Bible Societies' Greek New Testament*.

9. *Compare today's pericope with its parallels in other gospels.*

A tool that should be in the library of everyone who has the responsibility of preaching is a book in which the gospels are set in parallel columns, such as Burton Throckmorton, *Gospel Parallels*, or Kurt Aland, *Synopsis of the Four Gospels*. Such a gospel harmony makes it easy to see how the version of a story or saying appearing in the gospel featured in the lectionary this year compares with the versions that appear in the other gospels. Such a comparison helps you to understand the use that the current version made of its sources and to see the way in which the evangelist used the story to communicate his theological emphases. This is to say that you are to engage in source criticism and redaction criticism.

The basic conclusions of source criticism are simple and questioned by very few scholars. Matthew and Luke used Mark as a source. They also shared another source, consisting largely of the sayings of Jesus, that scholars call "Q." In addition, each of the two has material that is exclusive to it, whether derived from a private source or the product of the evangelist's editorial activity; Matthew's special material is referred to as "M" and Luke's as "L." John belongs to a stream of tradition different from that of the synoptic gospels and has very few duplications of material appearing in them. When the Sunday gospel is from John, then, there is far less comparison to make.

When we see how Matthew or Luke has altered Mark or how they differ in their presentation of Q material, we have important indications of their theological intention in telling the story the way they did. These variations, therefore, are some of the best guides we have to the meaning of a passage. They should be studied carefully. Some people have even found it helpful to use underlining, highlighting, or other, forms of notation on the pages of their gospel harmony.

10. *Note what comes before and after today's pericope in the gospel from which it is taken.*

In addition to the use they make of their sources, one of the main indications of the intention of an evangelist used by redaction critics is the sequence of material. The outline of the whole book can be considered an indication of its argument. Seeing where the Sunday passage fits in can give a good clue to what the evangelist is trying to accomplish by telling this particular story. For example, in Mark's account of Jesus' entry into Jerusalem in chapter 11, he does not have Jesus cleanse the Temple as the climax of the entry the way that Matthew and Luke do. Rather, he saves the cleansing for the next day and sets it between the story of Jesus' cursing the fig tree and that of the discovery that the cursed tree had withered by the end of the day. This "sandwiching" of the cleansing of the Temple between the two parts of the narrative about the fig tree suggests very strongly that Mark intended the cleansing to be interpreted in the light of the fig tree story. By the same token, the fig tree narrative is revealed to be a parable that is treated as an event in the life of Jesus rather than as a tale that he told.

11. *Fit this passage into the sequence of gospels in the current lectionary cycle.*

The evangelist is not the only party with whose intention in telling a gospel story we are concerned. Another is the church. There are reasons why just this story was chosen for this Sunday. (For an excellent discussion of the rationale of the current three-year lectionary cycle, see Skudlarek, *The Word in Worship*, pp. 32-37.) The congregation will hear this Sunday's gospel in the light of last Sunday's and this Sunday's will in turn be part of the context in which next Sunday's gospel is heard. All of this needs to be taken into account by the preacher.

12. *Discover the evangelist's special theological vocabulary.*

There is a strong temptation for contemporary readers of the Bible to assume that the words in its theological vocabulary mean the same thing as the same words mean in our modern theological vocabulary. There are, of course, inevitable overlaps of meaning, but there are not only major differences between the way certain words were used then and now, there are even differences between the way those words were used in different sections of the canon of scriptures. Most persons who have done any critical study of the New Testament know, for instance, that what Paul means by faith differs considerably from what the Epistle of James means by it and that the Epistle to the Hebrews differs from both of them.

There are, however, much subtler differences. The three synoptic gospels, surprisingly, do not use even such key terms as "kingdom of God," "Son of Man," and "Son of God" in the same way. To make sure that you are not importing Mark's understanding to Matthew's use, then, you will need to look up all the terms in the passage that are theologically significant. There is a considerable array of helpful reference books for this task. The nine volumes of Kittel's *Theological Dictionary of the New Testament* form one of the monuments of modern biblical scholarship, although they are getting a bit dated by now as well as too long and technical to use for every term that appears in a passage. Alan Richardson's *Theological*

Word Book of the Bible makes a convenient one-volume substitute. More recent than either of these is *The Interpreter's Dictionary of the Bible* (four volumes and a supplement) and John McKenzie's one-volume *Dictionary of the Bible*. Rudolf Bultmann, *The Theology of the New Testament*, is more useful for John than the synoptics because of the scholarship in the latter that has been published since he wrote. Redaction critical studies on the individual gospels are other good places to see how technical terms were used by a given evangelist.

13. *Look up the persons, places, objects, and institutions mentioned in the passage.*

This principle is very similar to the previous one and many of the same reference books can be used, especially the dictionaries of the Bible. Just as knowing the meaning of theological terms is necessary for understanding a passage, so is a recognition of the various allusions made in it. If someone greater than Solomon is here (Matthew 12:42/ /Luke 11:31), who was Solomon? Even more interesting, who was the Queen of the South who came to hear him? What is the relation of Galilee to Samaria and Judea? What are the differences between the Sadducees, the Pharisees, the Herodians, and the Zealots? How much buying power would a talent or a shekel have? How long is a cubit? What are the festivals all about that John says Jesus went to Jerusalem to attend? Most seminary graduates have at least a vague idea about the answers to all these questions, but a clear understanding could cause a particular narrative to snap into focus the way that a projected color slide does a second after it appears on the screen.

14. *Reflect on the affirmation the evangelist makes about Jesus in this pericope.*

One of the most extraordinary things about the way that Christians read scripture is that, although they may spend a certain amount of time asking what a passage means to them, they seldom get around to asking what the author intended to say in it, what point he was trying to make. Yet one of the contributions of form criticism to our understanding of the gospels is the recognition that each story or paragraph of sayings is the entire gospel in a nutshell. The reason that these individual units of tradition could be passed down by word of mouth for some years before any was written down as part of a consecutive account of the life of Jesus is that each contains an affirmation about Jesus that is ultimate in its implications.

Many examples could be cited, but a look at the "Controversy Stories" in Mark 2:1-3:6 should suffice. The story of the healing of the paralytic affirms that Jesus has the power to forgive sins, which his opponents knew was reserved to God. His eating with tax collectors and sinners showed his superiority to the dietary laws that occupied a prominent role in the strategy of the Pharisees for bringing in the kingdom of God. The failure of his disciples to fast was an indication of the uniqueness in history of his time on earth. When the disciples plucked grain on the sabbath and he said that the Son of Man is lord even of the sabbath, he was claiming to be superior to one of the holiest of religious institutions and to have authority greater than Moses. His opponents certainly were aware of these implicit claims, as may be seen in the reaction of the Pharisees and Herodians to his healing the man with a withered hand on the sabbath: they left the synagogue and began to plot to kill him because they recognized the threat he posed to the entire religious system that they held to be holy.

If there is such a basic proclamation in each pericope, does that have implications for preaching? In some languages there are grammatical constructions that "expect the answer *yes*." This question is obviously phrased to elicit such a response, yet what those implications are is not so obvious as one might think. A lot could be said for establishing a principle that the proclamation of a homily should always be the proclamation of the pericope on which it is based. At the same time, however, it must be recognized that such a principle would invalidate most of the preaching that has been done in 2,000 years of church history. Futhermore, it is even inconsistent with the use of scripture that is made within the Bible itself. Most of the theology of the New Testament, for instance, is based on a christological interpretation of verses from the Old Testament. No modern scholar would say that the meaning the New Testament writers get out of those verses is precisely what the Old Testament writers intended their first readers to understand. Yet Christians are bound to be convinced that Jesus fulfilled the deepest longings of

Israel, that what he was is what they would have hoped for if they had known enough to hope that well.

This is to suggest that appropriate insights may be drawn from scripture that are in addition to the point that a sacred writer was trying to make in that passage. Apt extensions of the meaning of a passage can be made. Needless to say, the criteria for establishing such aptness are numerous and subtle, and applying them calls for delicacy, rigor, and integrity. The only one of these criteria to be mentioned now, though, is that the extension be consistent with the original application.

15. *Distinguish between the use the evangelist makes of the story or saying, the reason that pericope was preserved in oral tradition, and the significance of that event in the life of Jesus.*

This step is closely related to the preceding one. It says, in effect, that even in the story as it appears in the gospel there is not just one meaning but three. Redaction criticism concentrates on the matter discussed in the previous paragraph, the affirmation that the evangelist was making. Form criticism deals with the other two, the reason the story was preserved in oral tradition and the significance of the event in the life of Jesus. Scholars talk about the *Sitzim-Leben*, the life situation, of a pericope. There are three such life situations: in the gospel, in oral tradition, and in the life of Jesus. One could even add a fourth that is the liturgical occasion for the reading of that gospel passage. And the meaning is different in each.

As an example, we may look at the parable of the Sower in Mark 4. In Mark the parable is related to the doctrine of the Messianic Secret and is used to demonstrate the point that parables were not illustrations or arguments Jesus used, but were instead designed to veil his meaning. Joachim Jeremias, whose *The Parables of Jesus* should be consulted before anyone ever dares to preach on a parable, says that the allegorical explanation of the parable was added by the early church during the period of oral transmission to turn the parable into "an exhortation to converts to examine themselves and test the sincerity of their conversion" (p. 79). Jesus, however, told the parable originally to reassure his followers who were discouraged by the poor response to their preaching, that "in spite of every failure and opposition, from hopeless beginnings, God brings forth the triumphant end which he promised" (p. 150).

Each of these three levels of meaning would be appropriate to preach from. (It should be noted that not all pericopes have three levels since some originated in oral tradition and others in the editorial work of the evangelist. Yet those that have parallels in the synoptics have an additional use in the thought of the evangelist for every gospel in which they appear.)

16. *Compare your interpretation with that of a few good commentaries and exegetical aids and revise your interpretations as necessary in the light of that comparison.*

By this time you have performed at your own level all of the activities that a trained biblical scholar would have gone through to interpret your passage. You could, of course, have taken a shortcut and consulted their books at the beginning of your work, but that would have made your own involvement and understanding of the pericope much more superficial than it is after this effort to wrestle with its interpretation yourself.

Something should be said about the commentaries to be consulted. All generalizations have their exceptions, but if one's commentary is over fifteen years old, it is probably not worth bothering with. The knowledge explosion is as characteristic of biblical studies as it is any other academic discipline and fresh scholarship makes for fresh preaching. The Appendix on Resources lists some of the better recent volumes on individual gospels. Some shorter aids can be listed here. Two single-volume works that are usually worth looking at are *The Jerome Biblical Commentary* and *The Interpreter's One-Volume Commentary on the Bible*. Homiletical aids that have good exegetical material include Reginald H. Fuller's *Preaching from the New Lectionary* and Fortress Press's two (soon to be three) *Proclamation* series. There are also good subscription services for homiletical assistance, such as *Celebration—A Creative Worship Service* from Kansas City.

Even if the authorities you consult disagree with your tentative interpretation and convince you that you were off on the wrong track, their exegesis will mean far more to you after you have already explored the issues raised by the text on your own. You will understand better not only what they say but also why they say it. Do not submit immediately to authority, though, like an arithmetic student looking up an answer in the back of the book or a mystery story reader peeking at the last page to find out "who done it." Make them show that their case is stronger than yours. When you become convinced that it is, then their interpretation will have become your own.

17. *Go back and read the story over again in the light of your study, yet listen for a coherent narrative while you do so.*

All of this study has been for the purpose of helping to understand the passage better. If it has not, you have wasted your time. Some clergy seem to act as though the biblical criticism they were taught in seminary has no practical use beyond protecting their gnostic status as professionals. Yet it is intended to be one of the most practical subjects that one studies. It is designed to help you understand what you proclaim so that you can proclaim it more effectively. Failing to use it is like counting on your fingers when you have a computer available.

Many of us have had the assignment of translating something written in a foreign language that we know in a rudimentary way. We start out by looking over the whole thing and seeing what sort of sense we can make of it from a sight reading. Sometimes that gets us pretty far, but we usually have to drag out at least the lexicon and maybe a grammar as well. We go through and look up every unfamiliar word and construction. Then we go back over the whole thing and discover that it makes much more sense than it did the first time. When we read our pericope straight through after having completed our exegesis, we should have a similar experience of greatly enhanced understanding.

Not only that. There should also be a much livelier appreciation of the story told. A lot of details that were vague before now make their contribution to the total effect. From all this we ought to be able to find something to preach about. If not, there is probably a serious spiritual deficiency in us.

18. *Now study the other lessons for the day to see how they illuminate the gospel.*

Some authorities so define liturgical preaching that a homily must be based on all the lections to qualify. Either liturgical preaching does not have to be that way or I have no particular investment in holding it up as an ideal. The ten to fifteen minutes available for a homily is seldom adequate for the gospel, let alone two additional readings and a psalm as well. Dragging them in can be quite artificial, since course reading is done for the epistle and it was not chosen with the particular gospel in mind.

There are, however, times when a phrase, point, or story from one of the other readings is exactly what is needed to back up the proclamation of the gospel.

The possibility is greater with the Old Testament reading since it was chosen with the gospel in mind. If you find something that really adds, use it. If not, let it go. In any case, you will probably spend a good deal less time in your exegesis of these readings than you did with the gospel, although the effort will be richly repaid in other ways if you can find the time.

III. Applying It To The Congregation

When you have completed all the steps outlined in
the last chapter you will know what the passage
meant to the audience for which it was originally intended. Your next task is to find out what it *means* to
your parish today. Merely to talk about what the sacred writer wanted to convey to his first readers is to
engage in historical reconstruction. The word of God
becomes living and active when it is understood in
terms of its implications for contemporary Christians.
The proclamation of the pericope has to be *applied* to
lives of the people who hear you preach. The entire
enterprise of preaching is predicated upon the assumption that there are analogies between the situation addressed by the biblical writer and situations
in your parish today. It is by pointing out those
analogies that you can illuminate the lives of your
people with the light of the word. In order to do that,
though, you have to study your parish. You have at
least as big a task interpreting it as you had in interpreting the gospel passage appointed for Sunday.
What follows are the steps through which you must
go in order to perform that task.

1. *Analyze your audience.*
We sometimes act as though meaning were an abso-
lute rather than a relative quality. "To mean," how-

ever, is a transitive verb. Words must mean *something* to *somebody*. In a similar way, we speak of certain things as significant, yet "to signify" has the root meaning of serving as a sign. What is significant, therefore, points somebody toward something. Thus a sermon cannot be addressed to the thin air with any assurance that something worth doing has been accomplished. An old evangelical term for a sermon was "the message," but messages have to be received by the persons to whom they were addressed and they have to be understood. Really to engage in preaching, then, means that we say something that we consider to be important to particular people, we say it to them, and we say it in such a way that they can understand it, will be interested in it, and, we pray, persuaded by it. For that to happen, we must know to whom we are speaking.

Even the smallest congregation incorporates representatives of a number of different groups. There are, for instance, persons of almost every age. Yet the preoccupations of young singles, for instance, are very different even from those of their own contemporaries who are married. The issues of life for young parents are by no means the same as those for their children, on the one hand, or their parents, on the other. Teenagers are different from kindergarteners and sociologists are even beginning to distinguish between the young-old (50-70) and the old-old (above seventy). Sermons that hold attention and that are helpful are preached by those aware of the range of concerns that occupies the various age groups that make up the congregation.

And, after admitting the validity of most that has been said recently about the danger of sexual stereotypes, it still must be recognized that some subjects will interest more of the men in the congregation than women, and vice versa. Marital status has already been alluded to as a factor in determining interests. Amount and kind of education is another. High school dropouts and Ph.D.'s do not usually have the same interests, nor, as far as that goes, do those with doctorates in botany and those with doctorates in English. Socio-economic groups, racial and ethnic representations, and, of course, those with more or less religious training, involvement, and experience will all need to be addressed in different ways.

Obviously, no homily can be written that will succeed in being equally meaningful to every member of the congregation, but the preacher should still remember that those who hear it will include all of these categories of persons and others. Perhaps the ideal is to aim for what is basically human, slant in the direction of a major constituency, and provide a few opportunities for others to be included along the way. And different mixes can be addressed on different Sundays. Yet at the beginning of every effort to figure out how that Sunday's gospel is to be applied to one's parish each week there should be a pause in which the diversity of its membership is recalled.

2. *Listen for resonances between Sunday's gospel and issues that have come up recently in conversations with parishioners.*

It has been said that clergy spend too much time answering questions that no one is asking. One reason for doing that is not knowing what questions they are asking. We cannot expect to preach effectively to people with whom we have no other communication. With the growing shortage of vocations not many priests have enough time for unstructured conversation with parishioners. After emergencies have been attended to, confessions heard, meetings attended, and liturgies performed little time is left over just to find out what is on people's minds.

Yet in precisely this hectic weekly round of duties there are numerous opportunities for discovering the issues that preoccupy parishioners, the things they think about when they lie awake at three o'clock in the morning. Since so many of the occasions on which they speak to us are times of anxiety and stress, what they say is much more likely to represent where their attention is really focused than their remarks on more formal or gracious occasions. Many Catholics have developed a surface affability as the way one speaks to priests that is at least as useful for the protection it gives them as for the deference and affection it indicates for those in holy orders. One only learns what they really think, what their true concerns are, when something causes the mask to slip momentarily.

Yet it is this genuine emotion with which the preacher must be in touch, not only in order to be able to speak about what people are interested in, but also in order to find the issues in their lives that are as serious as those dealt with in the gospels. We assume that parallels exist between the situation in the text and the situation in the parish, but the text shows us plainly what really matters and is not up for grabs, while parishioners are often reluctant to do that. If we are to apply the text, we must find that with which it corresponds. That means listening and listening of a special sort—the kind the psychiatrist Theodore Reik referred to as "listening with the third ear."

One of the reasons for beginning sermon preparation on Monday is to have several days in which the themes of the gospel are running around in your mind. While part of your mind is turning them over and over, another part is also reflecting on all the problems (and joys) of parishioners. If both of those things are going on simultaneously, then the time will come when the two parts of your mind will start speaking to each other. One will say, "Hey, what you have been thinking about is the same thing that I have been thinking about." When that happens, a sermon is on the way. This validates the point made by Bonhoeffer: "We should listen with the ears of God that we may speak the Word of God" (quoted in Chartier, *Preaching as Communication*, p. 44).

3. *Ask why this pericope was appointed for this particular feast in the calendar and how both are related to the total mystery of Christ.*

The relation between the liturgical season and the liturgy of the word is very well spelled out in the Introduction to the 1982 revision of the Lectionary:

The purpose of the homily at Mass is that the spoken word of God and the liturgy of the eucharist may together become "a proclamation of God's wonderful works in the history of salvation, the mystery of Christ." Through the readings and homily Christ's pascal mystery is proclaimed; through the sacrifice of the Mass it becomes present. (24).

The Introduction goes on to point out that "Christ himself is also always present and active in the preaching of his Church." The point here, though, is that the event commemorated in the Sunday's gospel is not one among many that are episodically and atomistically unrelated to one another. Rather, as the form critics have pointed out, each of the individual pericopes of the gospel is the entire gospel in a nutshell. If the implications of any of these stories is thought through thoroughly, it will be seen that the claims made about Christ are ultimate so that an adequate basis for faith would exist if one knew only that story.

Yet the stories are spread through the calendar to make up the Christian year. In this way the total mystery of Christ is celebrated in the course of the year, but it is also true that the whole gospel is celebrated each Sunday and whenever the sacrifice of the Mass is offered. The entire gospel is implied as much by the accounts of Christ's humiliations during Lent as by the accounts of his triumphs during Epiphany, or even Easter itself. Thus week by week we hear proclaimed and see made present the total mystery of

Christ, but always in one particular, concrete manifestation.

The calendar, then, becomes a guidepost pointing to which aspect of the total mystery is to be sought in our particular gospel narrative. If we were to look at the story by itself, some other aspect of the total mystery could appear to us to be the most prominent one. The selection of that lection for its particular feast, though, provides the context in which we are to understand the lection. Thus we are not at the moment engaged in a rhapsody of liturgical theology but are instead engaged with a practical principle in applying a gospel pericope to the lives of the congregation. The calendar is an indication to us of the aspect of the pascal mystery to be proclaimed through the recounting of this week's gospel.

4. *See what relevance this gospel has to issues before the church.*

The Introduction to the 1982 Lectionary revision goes on to say that the homily "must always lead the community of the faithful to celebrate the eucharist wholeheartedly 'so that they may hold fast in their lives to what they have grasped by their faith.'" At a superficial level this could sound as though all that the homily is concerned with takes place at the church during the liturgy. Living eucharistically and living biblically are much more comprehensive undertakings than that. The wholehearted celebration of the liturgy in response to the proclamation of the Word enables the faithful to live out their faith in every aspect of their daily activity. Their faith is not an isolated compartment of life that only gets opened during the liturgy. Rather, it is the principle that informs everything else that is done during all the week.

We have already seen, therefore, that preaching should deal with the issues that preoccupy Christians in their personal lives. It is also true that preaching is one of the means by which the faithful are helped to understand some of the questions that are being debated within the church. This is not to say that the body of Christ is to be polarized by polemics or that the church's magisterium is to be undercut. Rather, it is to say that Christian opinion on these issues must always be consistent with the gospel. Loyal Catholics hear authoritative spokespersons taking diametrically different positions on questions of faith and morals that have not been settled and they are confused about what faithfulness requires of them. There is no point in cataloging such issues because any list would be out of date before it could be published, but such issues do arise and the people of the church need perspective on them. This is not to say that each Sunday's homily should be the latest bulletin on some noisy controversy. Some homilies, however, should address such issues and each week the preacher should consider whether that Sunday's gospel offers badly needed perspective on an issue that is dividing the church.

5. *Think of issues in the local community, the state, the nation, or the world to which this pericope speaks.*

In addition to all of the specifically theological and moral issues debated within the church, Christians need also to know the implications of the gospel for the problems that beset our total society. Many such problems that the world at large does not address from moral or theological perspectives will inevitably be viewed from that angle by Christians. It is inappropriate, of course, to engage in partisan politics from the pulpit, but, on the other hand, an issue does not cease to be moral just because people vote on it. In running over in their minds the possible areas of application for the Sunday gospel, then, preachers should not neglect issues in the local community, the state, the nation, and the world.

6. *Decide which area of application—personal, liturgical, parochial, theological, ethical, social, or political—is most urgent.*

So far in our thinking about the application of the gospel to the life of the congregation all we have done is to list the various areas of life to which the gospel can be applied. Implicit to this has been a claim that all of these areas are not only legitimate areas for preaching but are in fact areas to which the homily must extend on occasion to be an adequate response to the gospel. Thus the question is not whether the homily should ever deal with such matters but only what it should deal with that week. To try to do all or even a few such applications in a single homily would be to make unfair demands on the congregation and also to risk incoherence through superficiality. So a choice must be made.

Which shall it be? There are two main considerations in making a decision. One has to do with the congruence of the application to the gospel that is being applied. A given gospel is just going to fit better with some areas of application than others and one does not try to make the word of God jump through hoops. The other consideration, though, is what that particular congregation needs to hear about most urgently. Sometimes a particular area of application will have to be chosen because it is so much in the forefront of everyone's thoughts. To speak of something else when they want to know what to think about that is irresponsible. At other times, though, an area of application will be urgent precisely because no one is thinking about it and they ought to be thinking about it. At any rate, a choice has to be made between the dozens of options and the homilist will decide to make one application rather than any of the other possible ones. The worst sort of homily is that which imitates Don Quixote's horse and "gallops madly off in all directions."

7. Determine what perspective this proclamation casts on the situation to which it is to be applied.

We need to speak a little more clearly of the process that was taking place when each of the areas of application was being considered. It was essentially a process of free association. It was described a little at the end of the second rule in this chapter, where one part of the mind was thinking about the meaning of the gospel and another part was thinking about personal concerns of parishioners. The gospel would not serve equally well as an approach to all such problems; only certain ones would have something in common with the situation in the text. The same would be true of all the other areas of application as well. Only particular modern situations would be analogous to what was reported in the gospel and of those that were, some would be more analogous than others. This is the matter of congruence that was spoken of near the end of the discussion of the last rule.

It is this observation of a common principle operating between the situation in the text and the situation in the congregation that makes possible any application of a text to modern life. Because the situations are similar, the perspective taken on the situation in text by the sacred writer may be appropriately transferred to the modern situation. Now is the time to identify that perspective and transfer it to the area of application. This is the time to ask, "Now if this is what the biblical writer thought about a situation like this when it occurred in his time, what am I to think about such a situation when it comes up now?" Obviously you are to have the same basic attitude, but what does that attitude look like when it gets spelled out in terms of the contemporary situation? When you have answered that you will know pretty well the point that you will try to make in your homily.

IV. Developing the Idea

The previous chapter dealt with deciding to which aspect of Christian life today Sunday's gospel should be applied. In other words, the chapter dealt with deciding what to preach about. This chapter concerns what to say about the chosen topic. Many of the old manuals in homiletics distinguish between expository sermons and topical ones. Expository sermons take a passage of scripture and expound it. Topical sermons choose a subject and discuss it. The technique advocated in these pages is a combination of the two. It assumes that a Sunday homily will always be based on the gospel for the day, but its aim will not be limited to explaining what that passage means. Rather, as the last chapter indicated, the perspective of that gospel passage is to be applied to one aspect of Christian living today, which brings a topical dimension to homilies thus preached. But even here the idea is not just to analyze a subject such as sin, grace, forgiveness, the resurrection—or, for that matter, Andrew Greeley's novels or world hunger. As our definition of homily said, its purpose is to move members of the congregation to accept the point of doctrine drawn from the gospel and to act on the basis of it. A homily, then, can never be just the exposition of a subject. It is always a call for decision and action.

Since the purpose of the homily is not just to inform the faithful about a subject, but is to lead them to insight, conviction, and action, the hardest part of writing a homily is deciding what point you are going to make for which you wish to solicit agreement and consistent behavior. There is an old cliché that distinguishes between sermons that have something to say and those that have to say something. Obviously the first kind are the only ones worth preaching. But how do you move from your exegesis of the gospel and choice of an area of application to an idea of what to say?

Another way of asking the question is: where do inspirations for homilies come from? Ultimately, of course, the answer is theological: they come from the Holy Spirit. But how do you get him to deliver on time? The question is not asked irreverently, but it can be very urgent for the homilist who knows that preparation time is running out and that he or she has nothing worth saying.

It does not take much thought to realize that inspiration for a homily has much in common with the inspiration of artists. Homilies are, among other things, an art form. In both cases (homilies and other works of art), the ideas seem just to come, to rise into consciousness. This is really to say that they are formed (at least from a human point of view) in the unconscious mind and delivered into our conscious thought later. What follows, then, are techniques for wooing a muse, for setting the unconscious to work and for persuading it to part with its accomplishments. Techniques for this vary considerably and each homilist will have to discover his or her own most fruitful ones. Most of those listed below have been suggested by other writers in the field of homiletics. The main thing I could add personally to their methods is: "When all else fails, take a shower!" That, at any rate, is how many of my own best ideas come.

1. *Think before you write.*

This is the homiletical equivalent to the card one has seen posted over telephones: "Make sure the brain is engaged before the tongue is set in motion." The point is not that a fully written out manuscript should be prepared for every homily. Some preachers achieve better results with one and others without. There are also many stages in between the two extremes using outlines, notes, or what have you. This is rather to say that you need to know the overall structure and sequence of what you wish to say before you try saying it. Some homilists use writing as a warming up exercise to get them started thinking, but they should discard the results of this and only impose on the congregation what they have thoroughly thought through.

2. *Let the idea percolate, incubate, and distill.*

If ideas are developed in the unconscious, they have to have an opportunity to develop. This is another reason for starting preparation for Sunday's sermon no later than the preceding Monday. After the unconscious has the fruits of one's exegesis fed into it and the basic decision about the area of application, it can mull over these while the conscious mind (with body attached) goes about a thousand other tasks. It operates much as the kingdom of God does in the parable told in Mark 4:26-29:

The kingdom of God is as if a man should scatter seed upon the ground, and should sleep and rise night and day, and the seed should sprout and grow, he knows not how. The earth produces of itself, first the blade, then the ear, then the full grain in the ear. But when the grain is ripe, at once he puts in the sickle, because the harvest has come.

Eugene Lowry calls this phase of sermon preparation "wandering thoughtfulness" (*The Homiletical Plot*, p. 17). My understanding of why my best ideas come to me while showering is that they were actually developed by the unconscious while I slept and the relaxed time of the shower gives them an opportunity to rise effortlessly into consciousness. Any student who has ever struggled to solve a math problem until late at night and finally gone to bed in frustration only to wake up the next morning knowing the answer has experienced the same phenomenon. One of the best ways to get ideas to cook is to set them on one of the back burners of the mind.

3. *Ask yourself questions about the issue.*
Sometimes the unconscious needs a little prodding. One way of going about that is to ask questions, all kinds of questions that help you to look at an issue from a number of different perspectives. This method

is easier to illustrate than it is to describe and an excellent example has been given in H. Grady Davis' analysis of John 8:31-36, in which Jesus has told his audience that the truth will make them free and they take offense because as children of Abraham they have never been slaves:

What is Jesus talking about? He mentions *freedom* and he mentions *bondage*. What does he mean? Bondage to, freedom from what? Is it political? Is it social? Is it intellectual? If not, what bondage and what freedom is Jesus talking about?

He mentions *truth* and *knowledge* of the truth. What is this truth? What is this knowledge of the truth? Is it knowledge of scientific facts? Is it a correct philosophy of life? Is it a truth about history and culture? If not, what is the truth Jesus is talking about? What does he mean by knowing the truth?

What does Jesus actually say? He says, "the truth will make you free." But he also says, "if the Son makes you free." Does he mean that these are two different ways to freedom? If not, what does Jesus mean? (*Design for Preaching*, p. 52).

This is only about half of the questions that Davis asked of this one passage and he was preparing an old fashioned expository sermon instead of the sort of liturgical homily with which we are concerned, but he does show how questions can be used to stimulate thinking.

4. *Look at each character in the pericope and ask what aspect of your own personality is like the role of that character in this story.*

This technique is borrowed from a method of group meditation on biblical passages that was developed by Professor Walter Wink. After the members of the group have done their historical-critical homework on the exegesis of the passage, they begin to look at each character in the story and ask what motivates that character. Notice that, on the one hand, this is not like traditional techniques of meditation that try to reconstruct an event imaginatively by identifying with the point of view of one character in the story. Nor, on the other hand, is this a psychologizing interpretation that guesses at what emotions lay behind the action of an individual. Rather, this technique depends on clearly stated roles, such as those of the Pharisee and the tax collector in the parable. Jesus' portrait of the two has left little doubt about where they stand. But this technique goes on to ask, "What in my personality is like the Pharisee?" and "What part of me behaves like a tax collector?" The inspiration for this method came from Jungian dream analysis, which assumes that all of the characters in one's dream represent aspects of the dreamer's personality. What makes this process so useful for homilists is that it begins with a correspondence between the situation in the text and the situation in the congregation. It already constructs, then, the hermeneutical arch on which the homily rests.

5. *Think of four or five persons who will hear the homily and ask what good news the passage implies for them.*

Another way of beginning to move from the exegeted gospel and the chosen area of application to the thesis that will be annunciated or the question that will be faced in the homily is to visualize several members of the congregation who are likely to be present when the homily is preached. Do not think of abstract types but do chose individuals who represent the groups who make up the parish. Margaret Sullivan may be a working wife and mother who sings in the choir, likes informal liturgy, and wonders how she can meet all her other obligations and conform to the church's official teaching about marriage and the family. Tom Giordano, who helps administer the sacrament, is in investments and has distinct reservations about the activities of some priests and religious in Latin American countries. Pete Rabenhorst is the best center on any basketball team in the parochial school league, lives in a high rise housing project that has a higher crime rate than some small cities, and thinks God is calling him to the priesthood. Mary Kowalski is lucky enough to be able to afford servants to care for her and even has a chauffeur who can drive her to Mass, but her memory cuts in and out and she is never sure whether she has taken her medicine, eaten her meal, or already told you that. When the proclamation of today's gospel has its implications worked out for each of them in the chosen area of application, what does it look like? (This technique owes some of its inspiration to an essay by Morris J. Niedenthal.)

6. *Remember that a homily is not just about a thought, but about a thought that makes a difference.*

As ideas began to flow, we need criteria to decide which ones may be worth keeping. "What difference does it make?" is a question that applies one of the most relevant criteria. It is not enough for the content of a homily to be orthodox or even to be interesting. You need to know that people will be better off for having heard it, better off in significant ways. The leader of the Methodist revival, John Wesley, gave the advice: "Preach as a dying man to dying men." This perspective came in part from his conviction that those converted would escape a burning hell that all may not feel so strongly, but there should be urgency about all preaching. It is achieved in part by asking of every thesis for a homily that you consider: "So what?" Will it give your hearers new insight into what it means to be a Catholic Christian? Will they participate more fully in the liturgy because they have heard this? Will they be challenged to live more confidently because of God's promise? Will their consciences be sensitized to another dimension of living out the implications of the gospel? One thing is certain: if the homilist does not think the homily is important, it is certain that no one else will.

7. *Look for a sense of discrepancy or ambiguity in the gospel, a feeling that something is unresolved—a "bind."*

This rule has much in common with rule no. 6 in chapter II: "Note any striking, unexpected narrative details, paying special attention to what is most difficult to understand or accept." That rule, however, had to do with initial reactions to the pericope appointed for Sunday's gospel, while this principle is employed after you have already decided what you are going to preach about and are now wondering what you are going to say about it, how you are going to approach it, what handle will allow you to take hold of it. In the discussion of the earlier rule William Skudlarek was cited as one who thinks that the hard parts of the gospel to understand are those which offer most promise for preaching. A similar point of view is held by Eugene L. Lowry, whose description of what it is like to get an idea for a sermon conforms most closely to my own experience of the birth of such ideas. He would have sympathized with the intentions of a Scottish preacher of whom I once heard. Old-fashioned Calvinist congregations in Scotland were reputed to be so well informed theologically that they only needed to stay awake for the first five minutes of the long and learned discourses they had come to expect from the pulpit. By then they would have ascertained if the minister was "sound" or not and could doze off with the assumption that what remained to be said was predestined. One pastor tried to shock his congregation into staying awake by beginning his sermon in this way: "I take my text from 1 John (the Scottish pronunciation would be "one John"): 'God is love.' It's a damned lie!" At this everyone in the kirk sat bolt upright. Such a beginning could not be sustained, however. The preacher went on to say: "But stay. Per-r-r-adventure we ha' been a bit hasty in our joodgment."

The point is that a very plausible case can be made for treating the statement that God is love as a damned lie. His chosen people, for instance, who lost half their number—some six million human beings—in the holocaust, Hitler's "final solution of the Jewish problem," have excellent reason to question the thesis. The inhabitants of the southern hemisphere of our planet, most of whom live near the Plimsoll line of the subsistence level, may also raise understandable questions about the self-evident status of the affirmation. Even St. Teresa is supposed to have said to God, "If this is the way that you treat your servants, it is no wonder that you have so few."

While the tactics of the Scottish preacher are not to be recommended, a more prudent use of such discrepancies between the claims made by the gospel and ordinary human experience can do much to lead a congregation into considering an issue at a far more profound and personal level than they ever have before. We feel some ambiguity when we listen closely to the extraordinary claims we make. We feel that ambiguity as a sort of "itch" about the human condition. We either come to see how the gospel offers a "scratch" for that itch or we end in despair. Anyone who is not confident that ultimately the gospel can make sense of the whole human predicament has no good news to proclaim.

Chicago *Tribune* columnist Bill Granger was infuriated by a statement by the editor of *Chicago* magazine to the effect that newspapers should be more fun. He observed sarcastically that

John Fink (the editor) has a point. While the newspapers in town load up their pages with horrible
stories about the threat of nuclear war, the collapse of
public housing, the horror of the schools, the death
rattle of the (Chicago Transit Authority), crime and
taxes and all sorts of things that are . . . well . . .
down, *Chicago* magazine is fun (4/6/82).

We live in a world in which all of these un-fun things
are aspects of our existence and we are not entitled to
faith and hope that do not take these into consideration.

This, however, is just one example of the sense of
discrepancy that can be felt. When such feelings
arise, they also bring a rising sense of excitement to a
preacher who begins to feel: "Now I'm on to something. There might be a homily in this."

8. *Seek out the issues that concern the deep memory
rather than the surface memory.*
This is the point at which we need to consider the
quotation from Urban T. Holmes that was made in
the Foreword:

The sermon or homily . . . has as its object the inscape of existence, not the landscape. Preaching is
not teaching. As an act of evangelizing the deep
memory, it needs to reveal to us the inner person, not
describe the externals.

Most of what is to be said in this relatively long
comment on a rule is to be an exegesis of that statement. Probably nothing else in this book is so important to understand.

What I want to correct here is an essentially intellectual view of the transformation in orientation at which preaching aims. This view, which I have advocated myself in the past, assumes that what needs to be changed through preaching are concepts, ideas. A sophisticated form of this theory can draw on modern learning theory and the sociology of knowledge. It recognizes that all organisms, especially human beings, receive far more sensations than they can possibly process. The result is a sensory overload that forces us to develop sorting mechanisms that determine which sensations are important enough to rise to the level of consciousness. Implicit to the existence of such a mechanism is a definition of importance—which, in effect, is a view of the universe, a rudimentary metaphysic. That view, which can be called our "fundamental thinking," is, in effect, our sanity and thus we have deep emotional investment in its maintenance. New data we receive is either consistent with that fundamental thinking and is thus assimilated to it, or is inconsistent with it and challenges it. When the mass of the inconsistent data becomes critical and the challenge is successful, our fundamental thinking has to accommodate the new data. In this view, the target of preaching is fundamental thinking. Preaching seeks either to reinforce or to alter fundamental thinking. This fundamental thinking, though, functions at the level of concepts and is thus what Holmes refers to as the landscape of existence, the externals.

He also refers to fundamental thinking as the surface structure of meaning and contrasts that to the deep structure of meaning. By that he means something like what Freud called the subconscious and Jung the unconscious mind. A basic axiom of psychoanalysis is that persons with emotional patterns they wish to change but cannot change experience that inability because they assume that the change can be effected at the intellectual level of concepts, when in reality the problem lies much deeper in the part of the mind that has a metaphoric rather than a conceptual structure.

Ultimately, humanity's interpretation of the forces of good and evil within its world and of the action required for survival and growth stems from this deep structure (Holmes, *Turning to Christ*, pp. 71f.).

This deep memory is the home of our dreams and of the symbols and myths that make up primitive religion. It is the world with which much in modern art and literature is concerned. It is the level at which depth pyschology attempts to effect therapy. The content of this metaphorical world is suggested to us by a number of clues: the person we fall in love with, the things we laugh about or cry over, the fears that haunt us in the night, and the folk tales and fairy stories that have been passed down by many cultures. This is the inscape of existence, the inner person, that Holmes tells us must be evangelized.

This means that the strategy of the homily cannot just be arguments, although logic has its role to play. Rather, since the things to be changed are the basic metaphors by which the psyche interprets reality, the tools to be employed are other, more adequate metaphors and stories. For the Christian these come from the Bible. As Holmes says it, "repentance is a change or expansion at the level of the deep memory. The truth that is Christ engages our deep memory. He becomes the dominant metaphor" (p. 74).

This takes us back to our definition of homily as a sermon that applies a point of doctrine drawn from that day's gospel to the lives of the members of the congregation with the purpose of moving them by the use of narrative analogy and other rhetorical devices to accept that application and to act on the basis of it.

Preaching is a doubly narrative medium because, on the one hand, it is based on a gospel narrative and, on the other, because it uses narrative analogies to persuade.

Not surprisingly, Jesus was the most effective preacher who ever lived and his most distinctive homiletical technique was the use of parables. While parables are first and foremost narrative analogies, they function powerfully as arguments, as Eta Linnemann has demonstrated in her book, *Jesus of the Parables*. She says that most of Jesus' parables were addressed to his opponents and that in a parable he offered an analogy to the situation they were discussing. To win their acceptance of the analogy, he would make an intial concession to their point of view, as, e.g., in the Prodigal Son, he admitted that the boy deserved everything he got. By this initial concession, his point of view became "interlocked" with that of his opponents. Then he could invite them to come around and view the same situation from another point of view, that of God. By forcing them to do that, he forced them to come to a decision between the point of view they had previously held and the new one that he held before them. By aiming to alter the metaphors of their deep memory, he tried to convert them.

From this we learn that a homily is not an essay, it is not an analysis, it is not a debate. Good preaching is always essentially narrative and it aims to influence the deep memory of metaphors rather than the surface memory of concepts.

9. *Limit yourself to an idea that can be treated in the available time.*

We are still at the stage of developing the idea for the homily and this is one last criterion by which to decide whether a particular idea is worth further development or should be discarded. Some points take a lot more time to communicate than others. Sometimes it is a matter of background information that people need in order to understand what is being said, sometimes it is a matter of the complexity of the concept itself, and other times it will be necessary to overcome a lot of resistance on the part of the congregation to the point of view that is to be inculcated. This means that the homily, like any other medium of communication, can convey some things better than others.

Sometimes when I am on the lecture circuit I make the rather feeble joke that I am a professor and professors are accustomed to thinking in fifty-minute units. A homily is also a unit with a given time span—ideally ten to fifteen minutes. The sermons of many famous Protestant preachers in the earlier part of this century were twenty-five to thirty-five minutes long, and in the late eighteenth and early nineteenth centuries, sermons that lasted several hours were not unusual.

Whenever a particular idea is being considered we need to ask whether the presentation of that idea adequately takes more time than will be available. If so, it should be rejected because either people will be held longer than they expect and get fidgety or the idea will be presented in such a truncated or allusive fashion that no one will know what we are talking about. Of course, it is also possible to have an idea that takes less development than we have time for. If we decide to go ahead with it anyway, then temptations to pad should be resisted with all the moral fiber that sacramental grace and the prayers of the saints have given us. An old formula for success in public speaking is: "Stand up, speak up, shut up, and sit down." Still, there is the possibility that the congregation will not feel like children who have been let out of school early, but will really have a sense that they have been shortchanged because they had a right to expect something more. A good idea for a homily, then, will be an idea that can be developed adequately in just the amount of time that is usually available.

V. Constructing the Homily

A. BASIC OUTLINE

1. *Write out your thesis, your purpose, and the response you seek.*

This list of rules is intended to function in many ways like the countdown that airline pilots use for takeoffs and NASA uses for space launchings. This is to say that part of its function is not so much to see that particular operations are performed but to make sure that nothing important has been overlooked. I seldom take a number of these steps in an explicit way, but a homily preparation process in which such actions are not implicit would leave too much margin for error.

For instance, I seldom sit down and actually write out my thesis, purpose, and the response I seek. The rule is one that I borrowed from someone else's book. But it is an extremely important thing for someone to do who is just beginning to prepare for preaching in a methodical way. When I was receiving my first homiletics instruction from The Rev. James T. Cleland, one of the things that we had to do for every sermon we handed in was to summarize it in one sentence. He said that if we did not understand what we wanted to say that clearly, we would have a very hard time making the point clear to anyone else.

Then, with a twinkle in his eye and his Scot's burr, he would say: "If there's a mist in the pulpit, there's a fog in the pew." Writing the thesis out is a very good way of finding out whether you really know yourself what you are trying to say.

After you know that, it is worth asking why you want to say that. What difference does it make in the life of a Christian whether he or she knows or believes that? When you know what you want to say and that it is worth saying, you need to know how you can tell if the message had gotten across. Most contemporary thinking about the writing of objectives is that they should be stated in terms of clearly observable behavior so that one can readily tell whether they have been accomplished or not. For instance, one could preach on the thesis that the gospel lays on us the obligation to feed the hungry and say that one's purpose was to make the congregation aware of the millions of persons who are starving in Third World countries. If one then stated as the response sought something about each member of the parish feeling deeply the tragic situation of so much of the world's population, it would be hard to tell whether that objective had been achieved except for gasps or tears during the homily, or someone's saying after Mass, "Oh, Father, that's so terrible." But if your objective is to get parishioners to sign a card handed out by the ushers with the missalette on which they promise to eat no lunch on Fridays for the next three months and give what they save to the Maryknoll missionaries, you can tell how many did it. But until you have specified what response you want made to your sermon, you will never know whether it was made or not.

2. *Prepare an introduction that is brief, interesting, and raises the issue.*

This rule, borrowed from George Buttrick, reflects an insistence of homileticians on the tripartite division of sermons that is as firm as Caesar's similar conviction about Gaul. The theorem is not so simplistic as an affirmation that they have a beginning, a middle, and an end. It is rather that they have an introduction, a body, and a conclusion. The real affirmation is that the way you lead your audience into your subject and the way that you tie it all together at the end makes a lot of difference in the way that people are able to respond to it.

Even though most priests recognize the etymology of "introduction" and know that it means a leading into, it is amazing how few public speakers seem to recognize that the function of the first part of an address is to enable their audience to get into the subject as quickly and deeply as possible. If you do not snag the attention of those who hear you in the first few sentences you utter, it is unlikely that you will ever get it. Yet you cannot use an attention getter that has nothing to do with what you really wish to say. As soon as you have finished the interesting part, attention will wander. And using something other than what you really want to talk about is an admission that you do not really consider the subject very interesting yourself. An introduction is a place to show that you take both the subject and your audience seriously.

Tried and true ways of involving hearers from the start include opening a homily with a question, a problem, or a difficulty. This starts their minds to working. It engenders curiosity. Another classic method is to tell a story, if that story is really related to what you wish to talk about. These techniques will be discussed with more precision when particular outlines, or, better, "strategies" for homilies are presented below.

3. *Consider in what sequence your points are most naturally and effectively presented.*

The standard textbooks on homiletics are filled with discussions of how many categories of sermons there are. Four basic kinds usually get listed, although various authorities make some of these four subdivisions of the others. The four, some of which have been mentioned already, are: expository, textual, topical, and problem-centered. For our purposes, they may be defined as follows: an expository sermon is a verse-by-verse interpretation of a passage of scripture in which application to the congregation is intermixed with the running commentary on the text; textual preaching seeks to deal with a shorter passage of scripture—often just a verse or a part of a verse—and to apply that to the lives of the congregation; topical preaching does not begin with a passage of scripture but with a subject—sin, grace, redemption, world peace, the ecumenical movement, what have you—

and discusses an aspect of that from a point of view that is consistent with biblical teaching; problem-centered preaching, also called "life situation preaching," deals with a topic, but one of a particular sort: a problem, whether personal, social, community, national, or international, from the perspective of Christian faith. As suggested earlier, eucharistic homilies do not readily fall into any of these categories since they presuppose the liturgical year and the lectionary, yet they focus more on a situation with which members of the congregation have to deal than on biblical interpretation.

In addition to these basic categories of sermons, various writers on preaching have talked about several patterns into which the outlines of sermons fall. Again, few homilies at Mass will fall precisely into any of these patterns, but it is worth listing a number as suggestions of sequences in which points can fall naturally and effectively. The list of patterns to be presented is drawn from a dated but classic textbook of homiletics, *In the Minister's Workshop* by Yale professor Halford E. Luccock.

(a) the Ladder sermon is one in which the points follow one another as the successive rungs on a ladder do. Each point builds on the one before and leads to the one that follows. A ladder sermon might, for instance, begin with a "lowest common denominator" concensus affirmation and then, step by step, move on to affirmations that are progressively more restrictive, so that the last point is the sharpest and most adequate statement of the issue of which the homilist is capable.

(b) a Jewel sermon is almost the opposite of the ladder. Far from having each point build on the previous one, the points are like the facets of a diamond that one sees while turning it around and examining it. The diamond cutter will undoubtedly know how the facets are interrelated but the more casual viewer will appreciated each for itself without seeing greater connection between them than that they are aspects of the same thing.

(c) the Classification sermon assigns persons or things to different categories. The application of the Parable of the Sower which compares various responses to the preaching of the gospel with the receptivity of different kinds of soil to seed engages in such classification and has offered the text for countless classification sermons. So is the sermon I heard in which it was said that life is like a hall in which there are four doors: wealth, power, fame, and Jesus.

(d) the Skyrocket sermon, according to Luccock, is not just a fizz and a bang, but is a life-situation sermon that begins on the ground in life, it rises up to a spiritual truth that illuminates the situation on earth, and comes down to earth again in several stars that light up different aspects of the situation on the ground. There are similarities between this pattern and one that I will recommend later as a natural pattern for a liturgical homily.

(e) the Roman Candle sermon "consists of a succession of statements or observations which follow without any particular design except that they are all related to the subject" (Luccock, p. 141).

(f) the Analogy sermon "talks about one thing in terms of another" (p. 142). The "great I am" sayings of the Fourth Gospel in which our Lord identifies himself as the vine, the light, the water of life, the Good Shepherd, and so on, offer opportunities for such sermons.

(g) a Surprise Package sermon makes a beginning in which the development and perhaps even the end seems entirely predictable, but then it takes an unexpected turn.

(h) the Twin sermon, sets forth opposing or contrasting aspects of one truth or passage of scripture.

(i) a sermon employing the Chase technique is one that does not start off by giving the congregation an answer to a question, but instead leads it step by step through the process of arriving at a solution.

(j) the structure of a Rebuttal sermon is obvious: it is an effort to refute a position advanced by someone else that the preacher considers to be false or dangerously misleading. Thus it examines the arguments and conclusions of the opponent one by one.

In the more recent literature of homiletics there has been less inclination to list such patterns, even though they do give some idea of the infinite number of ways in which thought may be developed. Indeed that variety has been the impetus for the change, because now there is a widespread assumption that each idea has its own natural way to unfold and letting this organic development occur seems more important than sticking to some arbitrarily constructed pattern.

As already indicated, these questions apply with special force to the liturgical homily. One of the reasons this is so is a matter of time available for the homily. In this ten or fifteen minutes you are lucky if you can take one point from the gospel and apply it effectively to the life situation of the congregation. There can be, however, basic dynamics to the way that such one-point homilies develop. In the two rules that follow there will be a presentation of two of these dynamics, one that I developed in another book and one developed by Eugene L. Lowry.

4. *Present your thought in this sequence:*
a) Do not begin with the gospel but start instead with either the situation to which it is applied that can set the congregation to thinking about the issue at stake.
b) Show that the situation in the gospel is analogous to the situation to which it is applied to set the congregation to thinking about the issue at stake.
c) Transfer the perspective of the gospel to the situation of application.

All of the steps taken up to this point lead very easily into this kind of presentation. The first step was to see what the gospel says. The second was to find an area of the life of members of the congregation to which that point could be applied. Next the way of applying that point was thought through. You already know, therefore, what you are going to say. The question is how to say it. And the thesis argued here is that you do not begin your homily by exegeting the gospel because the average person in the pew does not know very much about sacred scripture and is not very interested in it—as such. No, the sermon should begin with a presentation of the problematic area of life, describing that so that your hearers can accept the description as an accurate statement of the way things really are. This is the situation in which they find themselves and in which they need some help.

The next step is to describe the situation in the gospel so that they can see that it is analogous to their own situation. They are not unique. Things have happened before that have a lot in common with what is happening to them. This is where the fruits of your exegetical study come in, but use only what is necessary to show that a common principle operates between the situation in the text and the situation in the congregation. It is this common principle that justifies applying to the contemporary situation the perspective taken in the gospel on the ancient situation.

And that is what is done next. You will be saying in effect that if these two situations are indeed comparable, then the implications of the gospel for our own situation are whatever you have deduced them to be. In this way your people are led to understand their lives in the light of the gospel. This event will be seen in the light of the total mystery of Christ and become a part of what is celebrated in the liturgy that day.

5. *Or present your thought in this sequence:*
a) Upset the equilibrium (Oops!)

b) Analyze the discrepancy (Ugh!)
c) Disclose the clue to the resolution (Aha!)
d) Experience the gospel (Whee!)
e) Anticipate the consequences (Yeah!)

Eugene L. Lowry, who is the originator of this pattern for a sermon, rejects the traditional wisdom that says success in preaching comes from "telling them what you are going to tell them, telling them, and then telling them what you have told them." He believes, correctly I think, that much of the interest of a sermon is the suspense of seeing its plot unfold. His technique is a variant of the problem-centered sermon. He begins with noting a discrepancy in the manner discussed under rule no. 7 in the previous chapter. This discrepancy is not just important to the preacher in getting the idea for the homily, it is what the homily begins with. The listeners are caught up into the homily by the intrinsic interest of the problem. Indeed, the planning of the homilist may begin with the solution (what Lowry calls the "scratch") rather than the problem (which he calls the "itch"). But the homily itself always begins with the discrepancy, the ambiguity. Lowry is convinced that a sermon is, among other things, a dramatic literary genre that has its own basic plot. In this genre, as in other dramatic plots, everything grows out of the ritual of the initial conflict. It is the conflict that creates and sustains interest. That conflict is the discovery that all is not right in the world. There is a snake in Eden. There is discrepancy between the sense of the congregation of what Peter Berger has called the "OK-ness of life" and life as it is actually experienced. The homily begins, therefore, by upsetting the equilibrium of the congregation when the preacher calls attention to this discrepancy. Lowry's students refer to this stage of the sermon as the experience of "Oops!"

The next stage is to see what issues are really at stake in this perceived discrepancy. This calls for looking behind our surface behavior to discover the motives, fears, and needs that are the cause or causes of the discrepancy. It is assumed, therefore, that the source of all our problems is not so much in the area of behavior as it is in the motivation behind the behavior. That motivation has to be diagnosed correctly. This is perhaps the most difficult part of the homily, the hardest intellectual (and spiritual) work of the preacher, because one's ability to match up the problem with the biblical solution is determined by the accuracy of this diagnosis. This stage of the homily is called the "Ugh!"

When the true nature of this problem has been revealed through such diagnosis, then one can move on to a resolution of it. But—and this is one of the most distinctive aspects of Lowry's analysis of the homiletical plot—the resolution does not usually come from the direction from which it is expected. The theological reason that he gives for this is the radical discontinuity between worldly wisdom and the gospel. If there were no gospel, the human condition would be without hope. This means that the previous step which diagnoses the problem has to be stated from the perspective of ordinary human wisdom. The clue to the resolution is seeing the situation from the point of view of God rather than from that of ordinary mortals. This principle of reversal was intrinsic to the parables of Jesus. His concession to the point of view of his opponents was the diagnosis, but after his attention was interlocked with theirs, he performed the reversal that forced them to look at the same situation from a new perspective. Since the reversal is called a *clue* to the resolution, this step is called the "Aha!"

When the clue to the resolution has been disclosed, it will always be seen that the resolution is in the gospel. It is here that the Christian solution to the problem is presented. The virtue of Lowry's approach is that it does not put the preacher in the position of answering questions that no one is asking. The need for the answer is felt before the answer is given, so that when it does come it is perceived as the gospel, the good news, that it is. This experiencing of the gospel stage is appropriately designated as "Whee!" (Or, maybe inappropriately. The trouble with pedagogical devices is that they work better with some people than others.)

The final element in this homiletical plot is to anticipate the consequences, to see the implications of this insight for future living. Note that this is not a series of exhortations. Much that has sailed under the banner of preaching has been harangues or pep talks urging people to make greater efforts. There is always an implied Pelagianism to such efforts, an assumption that people were not doing better simply because they were not trying hard enough. The basic assumption of the gospel, though, is that unaided human efforts are inadequate to meet the demands of living. God needs to intervene in history and in our lives in a way that opens new possibilities for us. This stage in the homiletical plot, therefore, is to show what the possibilities are that were opened up in the experiencing of the gospel. The designation of this step is "Yeah!"

6. *Or, let the narrative determine the sequence.*

Another sermon pattern that has proved effective, especially in the hands of skillful practitioners, has been to retell a story from the Bible, enlarging upon it narratively, and making frequent application to aspects of contemporary life that parallel details of the story. This pattern has been used especially by some of the great preachers in the Black churches, but has been by no means confined to them. The discussion of deep memory above shows why this method is so effective. Nothing grasps attention so much as a good story. As noted above, Fr. Fred Baumer called his cassette course on homiletics, *Preacher: Storyteller of God*. Perhaps the best way of describing this method is to quote extensively from Dr. Henry H. Mitchell's important study of *Black Preaching*:

It is probable that the one skill above all others which can open the door to influence and service is the skill of telling the story in the dramatic, imaginative Black idiom.

As is true with all good story telling, the Black Bible story must first of all be a work of art in its own right. The teller must tell it as if the telling were an end in itself, even though he may intersperse asides to sustain the obvious relevance of the action in the story. At any time while the story is being told, the teller must be caught up in it as if he had seen it happen. In the best tradition of the folk storyteller of all cultures, he must play all roles and make the story live. He must so communicate the story as to cause his audience to feel as if they, too, are at the scene of the action.

And yet the story must never be told for the sake of mere entertainment. The Black preacher, like the writer of a play, has a message. Plays and stories are processes which engage the vital emotions of an audience, making possible a new understanding and a new orientation and commitment. No matter how charming the story or how captivated the audience, the Black preacher must take care of business and lead the hearer to do something about the challenge of this part of the Word of God. The response so often and so freely generated by this great art must be focused beyond the teller to the source of the message, and to his will for the worshipper (pp. 133f.).

As Dr. Mitchell says, storytelling is an art that is common to all cultures. It is also one which meets with a positive response in all. It is hard to imagine any effective preaching that does not draw on it to an extent. The point here, though, is that the basic pattern for a homily can be formed by following the narrative of the gospel.

B. FILLING IN

1. *Decide what information you need to make the situation of application vivid, real, and important for the congregation.*

Both the pattern recommended by me in rule no. 4 of the last chapter and that borrowed from Lowry in rule no. 5 presuppose that the homily will begin with a discussion of a situation that is of real concern to members of the congregation. Rule no. 6 of chapter III listed the areas in which such situations may fall as liturgical, personal, parochial, theological, ethical, social, or political. There is nothing definitive or sacrosanct about that list but it does show something of the range that responsible preaching will cover over a period of time. Sometimes the aspect of the total mystery of Christ that is being celebrated that day will be all that is needed in the way of application, and the homilist's aim will be merely to enable the congregation to participate fully in the liturgy that day. At other times the gospel will seem to offer hope and help to individuals who are facing one kind of difficulty or another in their lives. Sometimes there is an issue before the parish to which the propers speak. Or the universal church may be disturbed by an issue that the appointed lection illuminates. An important moral or ethical issue may be widely debated in the society at a time when the gospel offers a perspective important in arriving at a Catholic assessment of the matter. Or there may be a social or political question on which the church should speak out (just as there are others on which it should remain silent, at least in its official voice).

Whatever the area of application, if it is to be described in such a way that the people present can recognize it as their own situation, the homilist must know enough about it to talk about it intelligently. Since no one has universal competence, that means that a lot of homework will have to be done in preparation for this part of the homily. Since the day is long past when the priest is likely to be the only or one of the better educated persons in the parish, important issues of credibility are involved here. Often the laity will have followed reports in newspapers and magazines and will recognize misinformation when they hear it. If they do not find the preacher reliable in matters about which they do know something, they will have difficulty postulating such reliability in areas in which they are less well informed. This does not mean, of course, that information relayed in a homily has to be encyclopedic; it only has to be accurate and balanced. Yet certain graphic details will do much to enliven a presentation and evoke interest.

2. *Use only as much exegesis as is necessary to legitimate your interpretation and application of the gospel.*

Some clergy preach like functional fundamentalists; nothing they ever say in a homily suggests that they have any question about the literal historical accuracy of everything in the Bible. Sometimes, though, those who consider historical-critical exegesis to be an important tool in their preaching go too far in the opposite direction. They want to tell the congregation all of the information about the pericope they learned while doing their exegesis. Much of it will not be relevant to the application that is being made and few lay people find such data exciting for its own sake. Besides, the study of the gospel was not conducted so that one could garner every possible bit of information about the passage. No, we study in order that we may know what point the evangelist is making in that pericope. What is of concern, then, is not the information, but the significance of the information. And not even all of the significant information needs to be included in the homily. Include only as much as is necessary to get your point across or to show that your interpretation is valid. Otherwise we may find ourselves in the position described by Grady Davis: "Instead of a finished statue, we may offer our people the chips we made in carving it" (*Design for Preaching*, pp. 204f.).

3. *Scan the application for differences between the clerical and lay perspectives and then restructure from the perspective of your hearers.*

The life of the average priest is very different from the life of the average lay person. Whenever one began seminary, whether minor or major, at the theologate or earlier, as a religious or diocesan, at that point one's preoccupations became different from those of even good Catholic laity. After that, your basic necessities of food, clothing, and shelter are taken care of. While careerism and ambition are certainly not unknown among the clergy, they at least take different manifestations and operate in more restricted arenas. While a vocation to celibacy does not eliminate your sex drive, it does curtail severely the number of prudent outlets through which it may be channeled. It would be possible to extend the list, but doing so would only be to belabor the obvious. The point, though, is that we understand life in terms of our experience of it. And, when we try to apply the gospel to life, our inclination is to apply it to life as we have experienced it. Illustrations that come very naturally to priests may be very foreign to lay persons. Most of our preaching, however, is addressed to lay persons and so it needs to illuminate their lives instead of our own. This calls for enormous empathy on our part, an empathy that must be schooled by close observation, careful listening, and reading a good bit of secular literature. Even then, habit is strong, so it helps to look back over what we have put together and make certain that it is really appropriate.

4. *Check the chain of your argument for weak links.*
The story is told of the janitor of a large Protestant church who was cleaning up the church one Monday morning and discovered that the pastor had left the manuscript of his sermon for the day before in the pulpit. Picking it up to return it to the pastor's study, the janitor noted that in the margin of the typescript were hand written notes which proved upon inspection to be instructions for delivery. In addition to such directions as "softly" and "pause dramatically," he came across one that said, "Argument weak here. Yell like hell." Unfortunately, yelling is not enough (although the good pastor had at least gone over what

he had written and he recognized a weak argument when he saw one). Sometimes a point will seem more cogent when we first set it down than it does upon re-reading. When that happens, the only honest thing to do is to replace it with a stronger one or leave that point out.

5. *Decide what points need clarification, illustration, and emphasis.*

At this stage we are moving from an outline to a full manuscript. Now is the time to decide upon the relative importance of the various components of the homily and see that attention is given where it is needed and not allowed to dissipate on irrelevancies. The amount of time given to a point should be in proportion to its significance.

Sometimes a necessary step in the argument is a bit complex or abstruse. If the congregation's understanding of what follows depends on getting this point straight, then it is necessary to take as much time as is necessary to state the point clearly.

As indicated in our original definition of homily, the matter of illustration is crucial to the development of good sermons. More argument is advanced through narrative analogy than through closely reasoned expositions of concepts. Nothing perks up attention so much as a good story, and nothing is quite so persuasive as hearing the principle applied in an account of the lives of people. Illustrations may be drawn from a range of sources: the Bible, great litera-

ture, current fiction, TV shows or movies, the newspapers, memory (if it does not violate confidences or
embarrass individuals), or your own creative imagi-
nation. About the only source to be avoided is published collections of sermon illustrations. The story
told really needs to illustrate the point you are making and it is unlikely that anyone ever tried to make
exactly that point before. You need, therefore, to find
your own illustrations that really fit what you are trying to communicate.

Emphasis is given in a number of ways. Some of
them have already been indicated, such as amount of
time devoted to the point, clarification, and illustration. Others will be aspects of delivery such as volume and rate of speed. Still others will include the
choice of language; an artful phrase can be memora-
ble. Then, too, the use of quotations can help either
by lending authority to what is said or because
someone has anticipated you in finding the most expressive way of phrasing the particular point. And, it
should be remembered, emphasis is relative. To
emphasize every word in a homily is to emphasize
none since then they are all treated equally. The emphasis of some parts of a homily requires the de-
emphasis of others. Make sure that people have their
attention called most forcefully to the points in your
homily that you consider most important.

6. *Avoid generalizations and abstractions.*
Homilies that are about everything in general are
about nothing in particular. A sermon pattern men-

tioned by Luccock that he did not recommend was the "Magellan sermon," which goes around the world every Sunday (p. 154). One of the advantages of narrative illustrations is that they help keep the homily focused and concrete. Generalizations, including this one, sound vague, bland, and irrelevant. They seldom threaten guilty consciences and certainly do not offer hope to the discouraged. If you have something to say, say it. If you do not, for God's sake shut up!

7. *Make strongest points first.*

This rule violates the received wisdom on the subject, which urges one to build to a climax. The difficulty is that if you begin with your weakest points, by the time that you get to what you really want to say, you may have no audience left.

8. *Arrange your thought in a progression so orderly that it seems inevitable.*

The best book on writing clear English prose other than Strunk and White's *Manual of Style* is *The Reader Over Your Shoulder* by Robert Graves and Alan Hodge. They state a number of principles and illustrate the violation of these by quotations taken from newspapers and the writings and speeches of people who should know better. This rule is very close to their nineteenth principle, which is: "The order of ideas in a sentence or paragraph should be such that the reader need not rearrange them in his mind." To illustrate the principle they state the natural order of a familiar letter:

Acknowledgement of previous letter.

Comment on the points raised in it, in order of importance—the recipient's interest being given priority.

New information of importance—the recipient's interests being given priority.

Questions.

Postscript.

Then they describe the sort of writing that does not measure up to their standard:

It would take up too much space to analyse a mishandled argument in full. But readers will be familiar with the sort of argument that, if it ever commits itself to a statement of the problem, does not do so until a mass of jumbled evidence on subsidiary points has been adduced, after which it gives the verdict, and then evidence on the principal point, and then an irrelevant report on 'what the soldier's wife said,' and then contradictory statements about evidence on subsidiary points, and then perhaps a reconsideration of the verdict, and then fresh evidence, and finally a restatement of the verdict (p. 126).

They had written communication in mind, but what they have to say applies even more to oral communication, since hearers cannot look back over the material if they missed a connection. An ideal for written prose is that the reader should never have to look back over what has already been read. Considerations of the order of presentation are even more important for listeners who have no way to review.

9. *Make every element in the homily contribute to one unified effect.*

If the foregoing rule is observed, this one will be automatically. Yet there are differences of nuance between the two. This one, for instance, has some negative implications, the chief of which is to avoid what my teacher, Dr. Cleland, referred to as "baby kangaroos." By these he meant little sermons within a sermon, subsidiary points that were developed independently even though they had little connection with the main topic under consideration. When the issue gets mentioned in passing, the preacher decides that something ought to be said about that, too, and interrupts the flow of thought to do so.

This does not mean that there never should be digressions. In Greco-Roman rhetoric, planned digressions were considered to be one of the noblest ornaments in the art of the orator. In fact, St. Paul's rhapsody on love in 1 Corinthians 13 is such a rhetorical digression. As noted above, the secular use of the word *homilia* in Greek was to denote an informal, discursive talk characterized by digressions. The issue, then, is not whether there should ever be a digression; but whether the digression strengthens or weakens the total impact of the homily. The need for homilies to appeal to the deep memory rather than the surface memory often means that coming at a subject from the side rather than head on can be more effective. Just as in a mystery story, the audience does not need to know the significance of everything said at the moment that it is said. But here we are talking about carefully achieved artistic effects, not fumbling around.

The one unified effect also calls for consideration in such matters as word choice, illustrative matter chosen, the level of diction, use of the voice, consonance with the liturgy, and many other such factors. It is not too much to say of a good homily what Cleanth Brooks and Robert Penn Warren said of a good poem: it is a "well-wrought urn."

10. *Appeal not only to the surface memory with conceptual arguments, but to the deep memory with metaphors as well.*

What needs to be said on this subject has been said in the discussion under rule no. 8 in chapter IV. The issue was raised there as an aspect of developing an idea and now it needs to be considered as a part of filling in the outline, putting flesh on the skeleton.

11. *Build toward an end that is a climax or a resolution.*

A homily should conclude, not just stop. Another of the sermon patterns to which Luccock gives a negative recommendation is the Elephant sermon which, he says, "has a large trunk before, of introduction, description, illustration, or diagnosis, with such a little tail behind, of positive remedy or word of salvation" (p. 126). A homily, as we said, should have an introduction, a body, and a conclusion. The conclusion gives closure, it ties everything together so that all that was said may be seen to have been a unified statement. Conclusions can take a number of forms from summary to emotional crescendo. They are the place where the general statement is made personal, the message is applied to the lives of the congregation. By then the discrepancy has been diagnosed and the remedy is ready to be prescribed. Here the good news must be heard.

12. *Recognize that communication is not just a one-way street.*

The architecture of a church has always been an indication of the theological understanding of those who built it. The gothic and baroque churches in which there are large and elaborate pulpits to which one must ascend by a staircase were built by persons who placed great emphasis on the magisterium of the church. Homilies were regarded as words from on high. The role of the preacher was to speak and that of the congregation was to listen. Such an arrangement results from what Myron R. Chartier has referred to as a "conveyor belt" theory of communication:

. . .in which meaning is taken from one person's head and dumped with 100 percent accuracy into another person's head. To these preachers, words are the carriers of information rather than vehicles for the stimulation of meaning. The shortcoming of the conveyor belt theory is that it suggests that meanings are inherent in the words used or in the messages sent. Actually, one person's meaning is never identical with that of other persons, because meanings are in people's minds, not in the words they use (*Preaching as Communication*, pp. 60f.).

Anyone who has preached very long has had the experience of being told that a particular homily was very helpful to the speaker at that point in his or her life. Before we begin to preen too much, we ask what point in that homily proved so helpful. Then, to our surprise and embarrassment, we are told something that we do not remember having said. Much of what parishioners will understand us to say will depend on their personal context when they hear it as well as on their life history and general world view. When writing, therefore, we need to expect that what we say will be heard in as many different ways as there are people listening. We need also to expect that this personal appropriation of what we say will more often be an enrichment than an impoverishment of what we had intended.

In writing we should also remember that while we preach we will receive countless signals in body language and in other ways of how the faithful are responding to what we are saying. That means that we should never be so bound to a manuscript that we lose our freedom to respond to the messages we are receiving from the faces turned toward us. Indeed, many writers on homiletics consider such eye contact with the congregation to be so important that they suggest that a preacher never go into the pulpit with a written text. My own view is that the number of ways of preaching well is as great as the number of good preachers. Each needs, therefore, to experiment until she or he has discovered what works out best personally. But whether a manuscript is used or not, the preacher should prepare with an expectation of two-way communication while the homily is being preached.

As we shall note later, that two-way conversation needs to continue after the homily is delivered. Some can arrange for a discussion session afterwards in which people share the thoughts set in motion by the homily. Others will want to have "feedback sessions" with a special group that was asked beforehand to evaluate the homily. There are other techniques as well. These all help prevent preaching from being a one-way street of communication.

13. *Aim at leading your hearers to understand, to feel, and to act.*

A homily needs to accomplish these three things. First, it should help the congregation to know what the issues are. They should know what the alternatives are and what is to be said for each. They should know what is at stake in the choice between alternatives. All of that is a matter of the mind. The homily should see that it is well informed. But it is not enough to know what is going on, one must also care. Emotions must become engaged. People are to be called on to choose a side, take a stand, feel passionately involved in the outcome. And that emotion must be put to work to influence the results. The homily needs to elicit all these results.

One hears so many more bad speeches than good ones that it is easy to forget the power of really effective public speaking. Anyone who remembers the Second World War, though, will have little doubt that an address can lead an audience to understand, to feel, and to act. Much of Hitler's whole theory of government was that the person who was capable of moving crowds emotionally should be their leader and the hypnotic power of his oratory is still evident in old news reels, even to people who despise everything he stood for and do not understand the language in which he spoke. By the same token, we remember how the will to resist was drilled into the British people by the speeches of Winston Churchill; his voice provided the calcium needed for their backbones. And the United States, which had become convinced in a time of depression that "the only thing to fear is fear itself" by the voice of Franklin D. Roosevelt over a radio, was equally ready to respond to that voice when it called us to war. More recently, one thinks of how important the oratory of Martin Luther King, Jr. was to the entire civil rights movement. Speech can be a powerful tool in the hands of a skilled craftsman.

14. *Proclaim the good news rather than chide or exhort.*
There have been so many abuses of the privilege of preaching that the *Oxford American Dictionary* can give as its third definition of *preach*: "to give moral advice in an obstrusive way." How far this is from the definition given above that "to preach . . . is to proclaim the good news that in Jesus Christ God has

acted finally and decisively for the reclamation of a lost world" (above, p. 18). How eloquent St. Paul would have been in his disdain of those who have tried to turn the gospel into a new law.

From the New Testament on, Christian preaching has had two aspects, proclamation and paranesis, publishing the good news of Jesus Christ and spelling out its implications for daily living. And there is a good bit of behavior, even among the faithful, that needs changing. Thus it is not suprising that so much of our preaching is in the hortatory vein. Morris J. Niedenthal, though, has offered a distinction between the "ironic" and the "heroic" that makes possible a strategy of paranesis that is consistent with the gospel we proclaim:

The difference between ironic statements and heroic statements reflects different stances in truth. Ironic perception and statement acknowledge and affirm the novelty and surprise of God's grace. Irony calls attention to and celebrates the amazing grace of God which exposes religious pretension and which utilizes sinners in the advancement and fulfillment of his purpose. Ironic perception and statement are appropriate to a stance which affirms that God loves and justifies sinners. Furthermore, ironic criticism cuts so deeply not because it shows up our failure to achieve heroic stature but because it goes straight to our denial of ourselves as human beings. Irony therefore affirms human beings in the concrete actuality of each: a mixture of weakness and strength, cowardice and courage, sin and faith.

Heroic perception and statement on the other hand tend to become legalistic, because they glorify human courage, human self-willing determination, and human achievement. Heroic criticism cuts at the point of our failure to become what we should be ideally, not our failure to become what we are. It criticizes people by saying that they should be *more* courageous, *more* involved, *more* committed. Heroism therefore affirms only human strength and cannot accomodate human weaknesses.

The preacher needs to learn the distinction between the ironic and the heroic modes of perception and their statements. The ironic is open to the novelty of grace and its operations; the heroic on the other hand often becomes legalistic (p. 146).

The temptation at this point is to exhort preachers to become ironic rather than heroic in their approach, but such an attempt would violate the very principle it hopes to uphold.

15. *Equip the congregation to participate in the rest of the liturgy.*

Whatever other application of the gospel is made in a homily, it must never be forgotten that it is in the context of the eucharistic liturgy that the homily is preached and that word and sacrament are inextricably bound up in one another. The connection is organic: the homily is based on the gospel which is appointed because of the liturgical season. The total event of Mass with homily is occupied with a particular aspect of the mystery of Christ. What is recalled in preaching is made present and celebrated in the liturgy. While, therefore, it is perfectly proper to refer the main thrust of the homily to an issue for the individual, church, or world that lies outside the time of the liturgical assembly, that assembly should never be ignored. As William Skudlarek puts it, "We need to know why we should lift up our hearts" (p. 70).

C. PHRASING

1. *Thou shalt not bore.*

When you come right down to it, the idea that the most exciting message the world has ever heard can be presented in a way that makes it sound old hat and dull is mind boggling. There are probably only two circumstances under which that could happen: (1) we are uninteresting, or (2) we find the gospel uninteresting. In either case, something ought to be done about it. In neither area, though, can anything significant be done during the week that one is preparing for a single homily. Nor, for that matter, can much be done about the suggestions that follow for livening up one's speech. Developing an interesting oral style takes years, but each of the techniques has to be practiced every time a talk is put together. Practicing them this time will at least make this homily better than it would have been otherwise. For long term improvement, though, attention must be paid to those who use the language well. Reading poetry is one way to improve a prose style. Listening to people who speak well and analyzing what contributes to their effectiveness helps. A little judicious borrowing can even be excused. While some people have a natural ear for speech and thus a native eloquence, few ever become effective speakers without study and working at the task.

2. *Eschew technical, pietistic, abstract, or pretentious language.*

A multitude of linguistic sins is included in this list and it takes great charity on the part of parishioners to cover them all. Theology, like any other academic discipline, has its own verbal shorthand that can speed up conversation between those who know it, but those who have not been to seminary seldom speak the language. The problem is not that the concepts are too technical for them to understand, but simply that the vocabulary is unfamiliar. It is very good discipline in clarity for us to see if we can translate the concept into everyday words.

A distinction is presupposed between pious and pietistic. The simple and straightforward language of devotion is not offensive, but we are generally offended by the impression that someone is trying to talk a better game of religion than he or she plays. Then, too, language that is vague and theoretical leaves the whole burden of application on your audience. It forces them to test whether you are talking about anything or not. And any words you use just to impress people will succeed in doing so— negatively.

3. *Use ordinary language, the language in which your parishioners think their own thoughts.*

There was a time when elevated diction was thought appropriate for the pulpit, perhaps because it seemed to lift us into an awareness of God's transcendence. Such language seems less successful now, perhaps because recent years have disclosed so much corruption in high places that ordinary citizens have become suspicious of anything that could be an instrument to bamboozle. At any rate, I have an unscientific conclusion that people today are more likely to trust plain than fancy talk. If it really is the sort of language in which parishioners think their own thoughts, they will be more open to it, since the ideas will seem less like something that someone else is trying to impose on them and more like conclusions to which they could come independently.

4. *Strive for vivid, expressive, vigorous articulation.* This may sound like an impossible thing to do if the previous rule of using ordinary language is observed. Yet notice the expressiveness of the following passage:

When you come right down to it, there is no law that says you have to use big words when you write or talk. There are lots of small words, and good ones, that can be made to say all the things you want to say, quite as well as the big ones. It may take more time to find them at first, but it can be well worth it, for all of us to know what they mean.

Some small words, more than you think, are rich with just the right feel, the right taste, as if made to help you say a thing the way it should be said.

Small words can be crisp, brief, terse—go to the point, like a knife. They have a charm of their own.

They dance, twist, turn, sing. Like sparks in the night they light the way for the eyes of those who read. They are the grace notes of prose. You know what they say the way you know a day is bright and fair at first sight. And you find, as you read, that you like the way they say it. Small words are gay. And they catch large thoughts and hold them up for all to see, like rare stones in rings of gold, or joy in the eyes of a child. Some make you feel, as well as see; "the cold deep dark of night, the hot salt sting of tears."

Small words move with ease when big words stand still—or, worse, bog down and get in the way of what you want to say. There is not much, in all truth, that small words will not say—and say quite well (Joseph A. Ecclesine, *Printer's Ink*).

The astute reader will have noticed that no word in this passage has more than one syllable. Measurements of the reading level of passages of prose rely on only two indicators: the number of syllables in words and the number of words in sentences. The goal of plain, vigorous prose is not impossible; it just takes discipline.

5. *Revise what you have written.*

A card published by the printing house of a religious community has the legend "I am infallable" with the second "a" of infallible crossed out and replaced with an "i" and the insertion of the word "almost." The rest of us do use the erasers on our pencils or the correction fluid or tape on our typewriters. That means that when we have finished a manuscript for a homily, we should read it over. Ideally we will do so just after we have finished and then some hours later we will do it again. The first time will be just to catch the obvious errors and make marginal revisions. By the second revision, though, we may have a little emotional distance on what we have written and be able to think of a better way of saying what we want to get across. We need to do that re-reading, therefore, when we still have time to put some of these good ideas for revision into practice. It is said that a recent President did not have time to look over an example of his speechwriter's art until he had actually to deliver it. In the speech was a joke he had not heard before and thought was immensely funny. He thus suffered the embarrassment of appearing to laugh inordinately at his own joke. Worse embarrassments await the homilist who never looks at his manuscript until he mounts the pulpit.

6. *Make clarity your first goal.*

This goal has been articulated in different ways at several stages in the homily preparation process, but it cannot be stressed too often. Perhaps an example of the difference that clear expression makes will offer encouragement to make the effort. The following piece of gobbledygook was written by "someone in the human resources department of a middle-sized state":

It is recommended that the focus, scope and purpose be clearly delineated and understood. Then, with the existing resources, the restructuring of the developmental process will be guided by the central concepts of the previously stated management philosophy. Specific functional and adminstrative activities, service outputs, and staff capacity development will be defined as real need demands are anticipated or identified. Armed with this real need information, a working management tool can be accurately designed through the use of the proposed management model.

Compare that paragraph with one written by the great authority on management, Peter Drucker:

It is not possible to manage, in other words, unless one first has a goal. It is not even possible to design the structure of an organization unless one knows what it is supposed to be doing and how to measure whether it is doing it.

Now, let's hear it for clarity!

7. Use correct grammar.

There are in every parish persons who know how English is correctly written and spoken and it sets their teeth on edge to encounter solecisms from the clergy. Many would be more forgiving if one fell into one of the classical christological heresies or broke a priestly vow in not too shocking a fashion. Nothing will make them lose the train of your thought and go off on one of their own quite so easily. Simple charity requires that one not offend them gratuitously.

8. Develop a clean English style.

The simplest guide to achieving that is to master the

manual from which this one takes its format: William Strunk, Jr. and E.B. White, *The Elements of Style*.

9. *Write for the ear rather than the eye.*
There are many differences between good oral and good written communication, too many to be discussed here. As an indication of the kinds of differences, though, we can look at those compiled by H. Grady Davis, who sets forth rules about words and rules about long sentences. The rules for words are:

If he is to write for the ear:

1. The preacher should learn to express himself in *as few words as possible*.

2. He should learn to use *words that sound well together*.

3. He should cultivate a preference for *short, strong, clear, familiar words*.

4. He should cultivate a preference for *sensuous rather than abstract, and specific rather than general words*.

5. He should rely on *strong nouns and verbs* to carry the weight of his thought.

Now the successful use of longer sentences depends on the observance of these basic principles.

1. The first factor is the *skeletal structure* of the sentence. The basic structure of the good longer sentence is logical, uncluttered, obvious.

2. A second factor, *connecting words*, is closely related to the first. The connecting words show the relation between structural parts of the sentence and mark the transition from one to another.

3. A third factor is *correspondence of parts*, of the phrases within a clause and of the clauses within a sentence. This means parallel construction and repeated construction.

4. A fourth factor is *co-ordination*. It means joining together elements of equal rank, words, phrases, and clauses, adding one to another with or without conjunctions.

5. A fifth factor is the *length of inner parts* of the sentence. Here is a difference between writing for the ear and for the eye. The ear cannot manage an element within the sentence that grows too long.

6. A final factor is that of the positions of *natural strength* in the sentence. The strongest places in a long sentence, as in a short one, are the beginning and the end. (*Design for Preaching*, pp. 265-93).

The entire discussion by Davis is very helpful and would repay any speaker's reading.

10. *Jerk wandering attention back.*
As we all know from our own attempts to listen to other speakers, it is hard to keep one's attention focused on what is being said. The experienced preacher will know this and include efforts to regain attention at points where it is likely to flag. Any sustained argument is likely to lose hold on some of the

audience. So is the prolonged use of one tone of voice. Other danger spots can be recognized by a loss of eye contact. A change of pace, an alternation of voice level, a little comic relief, telling a story—these and other techniques can be used to bring wandering sheep back into the fold.

11. *Use humor appropriately.*

Humor is a subject on which homiletical authorities diverge. Some say that it is inconsistent with the solemnity of the task of preaching. Since Jesus used it as a very effective tool, though, one assumes that the disciple is not greater than his Lord. Sometimes, though, what passes for preaching does not appear to differ materially from the routine of the standup comic. Surely the preacher should have something serious to say. Perhaps the best rule is to say that it should never become an end in itself. It must advance the argument of the homily rather than interrupt it. Humorous stories can sometimes make telling points very effectively. Probably, though, most of the humor that is injected into homilies should not be in the form of jokes told. Humorous turns of phrases are less likely to divert attention and more likely to reinforce a point. Irony can be quite telling. In trying to steer a middle course between being a buffoon and a sobersides, the criterion to remember is that the humor must always be a means to an end rather than an end in itself.

12. *Avoid embarrassing references to individuals.*

This is not quite to say that no one in the congregation should ever be mentioned from the pulpit, but it comes close. Certainly no one should ever be criticized or held up to ridicule. Something regarded as harmless humor or teasing by the preacher may not be so regarded by the butt of it. Even efforts to hold up a member of the parish as an example can misfire, either because the person preferred anonymity or because envy might be inspired.

13. Use self-disclosure discreetly.

When it comes to talking about oneself in a homily, you are almost in a damned if you do and damned if you don't situation. All preaching that is worthwhile has an element of testimony, or personal witness, to it. It helps the congregation to know that the herald believes the good news. The preacher's faith makes the gospel more credible to those in the pew. Yet at the same time, too frequent self-reference sounds like either boasting or self-absorption. One trend in recent years has been very upsetting for the faithful. In seminary, especially during Clinical Pastoral Education but at other times as well, those preparing for ordained ministry have been praised for taking risks by sharing their pilgrimage, their faith and their doubts. Such revelations which elicit praise in seminary, can be very threatening to the laity in a parish. They prefer teachers of the faith who are rock-solid so they can be a firm support in times when the laity have doubts. This picture can be exaggerated, but there have been many newly ordained clergy who have discovered that the behavior that won them approval in seminary is not always the behavior that has the same effect in the parish.

14. *Anticipate the effect of what you say on your hearers.*

What is called for here is empathy in advance. You can mean something one way that can be understood by those who hear you in a very different way. At the lowest and probably least harmful level, this can be no more than unintended double meanings, one of which is off color. And, because of the very solemnity of the occasion, nothing is as funny elsewhere as it is in church. Sometimes a preacher makes a slighting remark about a belief or religious practice that means a great deal to someone in the congregation. Even more likely to produce fireworks is a statement that makes light of the political convictions of parishioners. This is not to say that a priest should never say anything with which anyone can disagree. Far from it, but the way such things are said is very important. One must always take the persons with whom one disagrees very seriously and treat them with respect. As children of God they should expect no less from those who claim to represent Christ. Furthermore, clergy get into enough hot water inevitably and they do not need to increase the supply when they can avoid it by simply thinking about how what they say will sound to someone else.

15. *Stop on time.*
Nuff said.

VI. Delivering the Homily

One can have the best homily in the world and see it go flat because of the way in which it is delivered. The following rules point out some of the more obvious pitfalls.

1. *Do not read.*

The danger in preaching from a full manuscript is that you may find it easy to read it word for word. Eye contact is lost, body language responses from the congregation are missed, and people tend to read with less expression than they use in their ordinary speech. This is not so say, however, that one should never use a full manuscript in the pulpit. With practice you can develop a technique of dropping your eyes momentarily at the beginning of a sentence. By the time that you have written the manuscript, revised it, and gone over it several times, it should be familiar enough for you to follow it very closely with just these glances at the page. Often the congregation will not even know the manuscript is there. The chief advantages in using a manuscript are that the homily will be more tightly organized, more carefully phrased, and easier to keep within an alloted time. The chief disadvantage is that something of rapport with the congregation is inevitably lost.

2. *Do not ramble in undisciplined extempore.*

Some clergy assume that the only alternative to preaching from a full manuscript is to be totally unprepared. It is hard, though, for a congregation to take a homily more seriously than its preacher takes it. If it is not important enough for the one who delivers it to prepare, then it is not important enough for those in the congregation to listen to. Most of the many steps in preparation that have already been listed are as necessary in extempore preaching as they are in preaching from a manuscript. Furthermore, these are not the only alternatives. Some clergy preach from notes that remind them of the basic outline of what they wish to say. These may also include key phrases. Others write out the whole homily and then make notes from it that they use. There are probably still some who memorize the entire text, a practice that used to be more common. Others work to get the sequence of their thought so inevitable that they will not need notes when they speak. A good deal of experimentation is needed to discover what style works best for a given individual, but depending on the inspiration of the moment does not work well for anyone. One has no right to make the word of God appear boring.

3. *Project your voice without shouting.*

No matter how good your thought is and how well you have phrased it, it does no good unless people can hear it. Since priests do a lot of their work by public speaking, most have learned to manage adequately. For those who have not, there is always the possibility of finding a good voice teacher and taking lessons. Unless you do, much of your ministry is doomed to being ineffectual. It is to be hoped that those who speak too loudly will have friends who love them well enough to tell them. It is hard for anyone not to recoil from assaults on the ears.

4. *Become aware of your gestures and mannerisms and adjust them appropriately.*

Many seminaries these days use video taping equipment in their homiletics classes. This means that the prayer of Robert Burns, "O wad some Pow'r the giftie gie us/To see oursels as others see us," has finally been answered. How many seminarians have been surprised to learn that whenever they were speaking or practicing for presiding at the liturgy (what we used to call "dry runs"), they had a tendency to rock back and forth from their heels to their toes or that the only gesture they customarily made was to use their hands to describe the shape of a basketball in the air. And others have seen that they began by taking a tight grip on the edges of the pulpit and held on for dear life until the homily was over. Since most gestures and mannerisms are unconscious, the only hope for those who have not had the benefits of such technology is to ask a group of parishioners to watch them over a period of time and report to them what they do. In secondhand bookstores can be found manuals of elocution from the turn of the century with illustrations of the appropriate gesture for every emotion. Our age is suspicious of such melodrama, but a few well-executed gestures can add real emphasis to a homily. And we need to know about our mannerisms, because they can be very distracting.

5. *Call attention to what is being proclaimed rather than to the proclaimer.*

The gospels make it very clear that there are few things more contrary to the religion of Jesus than the self-importance of religious functionaries.

6. *Make each proclamation a testimony.*

There is an old saying to the effect that "you can't sell what you haven't bought." There are a lot of con men around who can question that, and religion has always been a fertile field for charlatans to work in. Even liars can say true things. When John Wesley, the founder of the Methodists, was awaiting conversion, he was advised by the Moravian pastor Peter Boehler to "preach faith until you have faith and then preach faith because you have faith." Yet there is something about the authenticity of a statement of a deeply held commitment that is hard to resist. As Robert Bellah said, no revolutionary can bring the future in whose life the future is not already present. All of this is to say that a homily is, among other things, a reflection of the spiritual life of the priest.

7. *Make each homily an address, an act of communication, a transaction between the homilist and the congregation.*

The verb traditionally used with sermons or homilies is "to deliver." In our changing social world, not as many things are delivered as used to be. When I was a boy, though, grocery orders were phoned in and brought to the house in a panel truck. And I even spent a few days as a Western Union telegram boy, delivering messages on my bicycle. To those who have participated in such transactions, it is axiomatic that no one has made a delivery until the order has been received. The onus was on the deliverer as much as on a process server. By the same token, the preacher's responsibility is not merely to say something or even to say something religious and significant, but to say something to somebody so that they will hear it and can understand it and act on it. Thus those who preach must remember that what is at stake are the lives of the persons who hear them. No homily has been delivered until its message has been received.

8. *Do not drop your voice at the end of sentences.*
This refers to the most common fault of those who speak in public and the result is that the meaning of much that they say is lost. Beyond that there is really little to be said about it except, "Don't do it."

9. *Avoid liturgical cadences.*
This refers to what someone has called a "stained-glass" voice, a sort of holy tone that some clergy affect while performing their duties in public worship. Such tones are common to many societies and are even cultivated in some. Henry Mitchell, for instance, says that it is used by many Black preachers in the inspirational climax at the end of a sermon,

but he insists that it cannot be used effectively by anyone for whom it is not a natural style of language (*Black Preaching*, pp. 163-67). Anyone who has heard examples of the sort of preaching he is talking about knows what virtuoso performances they can be. But in congregations where it is not a natural style of language, a special "holy tone" is generally thought to be hypocritical. Lay people generally prefer clergy who have the same way of speaking inside and outside of church.

10. *Treat microphones and amplifiers with distrust.*

When you can get by without a public address system, do. It is always hard to be certain whether one is working or not, or on or off. And it seems that more often than not, when you get the volume turned high enough to be clearly heard, then you start getting feedback that causes raucous whines. It is certainly wise to test any system over which you are going to be speaking before the time comes to use it. In fact, it is a good idea to stand in any new pulpit from which you are to preach just to "try it on for size" and get the feel of what it will be like preaching from there. Do not let yourself in for unnecessary surprises. To say one ameliorating word in favor of sound systems: they do allow a greater range of inflection with less vocal effort.

11. *Arrange for accurate and representative feedback.*

Almost the only opportunities most clergy get for evaluation of their preaching is what people say at the church door or, if another priest on the staff hears you, what might be said in the rectory. Being told, "Nice sermon, Father," or "I enjoyed your talk," gives one very little sense of areas in which to work for improvement. If you really want to work on improving your preaching, you have to arrange for more accurate and detailed responses.

Anyone who has a class or group that meets to discuss the homily has an opportunity at least to know whether the intended message got across, even if feedback is not the purpose of the discussion. Many clergy, though, have found it helpful to have a small group that has agreed to be present when they preach, listen carefully, and meet together with them afterwards to say as honestly as possible what they felt to be successful and what they felt to be less successful in the homily. Sometimes this group has a rotating membership so that additional reactions can be heard. In any case, it is a good idea to have a diverse group that represents different constituencies in the parish, since what goes over well with one group may miss another entirely.

There are also ways in which clergy can evaluate their own preaching. The usefulness of video tape for this purpose has already been mentioned and, in parishes that can afford it and have other uses for it, it may be a wise investment. Almost anyone can afford a cassette tape recorder, though, so almost every priest can hear what he sounded like even if he cannot see what he looked like.

When you have begun to evaluate your last homily, you have already begun to work on the next, since the only reason for going back over what you did last time is to make it possible to do better next time. Thus the work never ends. Nor should it, since to us has been given the high task of helping men and women understand their lives from the perspective of the God who made them, has redeemed them, and seeks to have them inherit all that he has prepared for them.

Resources

An adequate library is as necessary to the preacher as a well-filled tool box is for a carpenter or auto mechanic. The list of books that follows has a twofold purpose: it is both to acknowledge indebtedness for many of the thoughts in the preceding pages and to list books that should form the core of a preacher's library. Not all books on the list belong to both categories, although a surprising number of them do. In general, though, it can be said that the average parish priest will not need as many books on how to preach as are listed below, although all should have several. Most of the other books catalogued below should be regarded as essential and a systematic plan for acquiring those not already possessed should be set in motion.

Preaching

Fred Baumer CPPS, *Preacher: Storyteller of God* (Kansas City: National Catholic Reporter, 1981). This is not a book but a set of cassettes on which the professor of preaching at Chicago's Catholic Theological Union offers many helpful suggestions on preaching. Since Baumer and Skudlarek are among the few Roman Catholics who have discussed preaching from the practical point of view, their works will be especially helpful to most of the readers of this book.

H. Grady Davis, *Design for Preaching* (Philadelphia: Fortress Press, 1958). This is a classic textbook by a Luthern homiletics professor that goes into more detail about each stage of sermon preparation than most of the works listed. It encourages craftsmanship in preaching.

Simon Tugwell OP, *The Way of the Preacher* (London: Darton, Longman & Todd, 1979). In some way this deals more with the Domincan Order than the preparation and delivery of homilies, but it does have concern with the activity that gives the order its name.

William Skudlarek OSB, *The Word in Worship: Preaching in a Liturgical Context*, "Abingdon Preacher's Library," (Nashville: Abingdon, 1981). Good statement of the role of preaching in liturgical theology as well as an excellent discussion of the rationale of the new lectionary cycle.

Eugene L. Lowry, *The Homiletical Plot* (Atlanta: John Knox Press, 1980). The best treatment I have seen of how sermon ideas develop and a good pattern or "plot" for the sort of homilies discussed in this book.

Edmund A. Steimle, Morris J. Niedenthal, and Charles L. Rice, *Preaching the Story* (Philadelphia: Fortress Press, 1980). A good treatment of the narrative shape of preaching in a collection of essays and examples by these three editors and others.

Halford E. Luccock, *In the Minister's Workshop*, "Notable Books on Preaching" (Grand Rapids: Baker Book House, 1977, originally published in 1958). One of the true classics in the field. Slightly dated but still very useful.

O.C. Edwards, Jr., *The Living and Active Word: One Way to Preach from the Bible Today* (New York: Seabury Press, 1975). An earlier effort in which I tried to develop a particular homiletical pattern.

Henry H. Mitchell, *Black Preaching*, "Harper's Minister's Paperback Library" (San Francisco: Harper & Row, 1979, originally published 1970). An exciting analysis of one of the liveliest homiletical traditions around (although some Black theologians disagree with Mitchell's findings).

Myron R. Chartier, *Preaching as Communication: An Interpersonal Perspective*, "Abingdon Preacher's Library" (Nashville: Abingdon, 1981). An effort to draw on modern communications theory as a resource for preaching (although I have been told that it does not reflect the latest research in communications).

Ronald E. Sleeth, *Persuasive Preaching* (Berrien Springs, Mich.: Andrews University Press, 1981, originally published 1956). Helpful hints from one of the real old pros.

Clement Welsh, *Preaching in a New Key: Studies in the Psychology of Thinking and Listening* (Philadelphia: Pilgrim Press, 1974). A masterly discussion of the relation of learning theory to the strategy of preaching by the Warden of the Episcopal Church's College of Preachers.

The Bishop's Committee on Priestly Life and Ministry, *Fulfilled in Your Hearing: The Homily in the Sunday Assembly* (Washington, D.C.: United States Catholic Conference, 1982). An excellent official document that was still in manuscript at the time of this writing.

Proclamation, series 1 & 2, published by Fortress Press in Philadelphia. Each series is a set of twenty-four short booklets which comprise a commentary on the three-year lectionary cycle, with about a printed page of exegesis and another of suggestions for homiletical development done by some of the best known Scripture scholars and preachers in the country. A third series is soon to appear in which both exegesis and homiletical development will be written by the same person.

R.H. Fuller, *Preaching the New Lectionary: The Word of God for the Church Today* (Collegeville, MN: The Liturgical Press, 1975). A single-volume commentary on the new lectionary originally appearing in *Worship* magazine and written by a distinguished New Testament scholar.

Celebration—A Creative Worship Service. P.O. Box 281, Kansas City, MO 64141. A subscription service of material helpful in the preparation of homilies.

Biblical Scholarship

Reference Books

Bruce M. Metzger, *A Textual Commentary on the Greek New Testament* (London/New York: United Bible Societies, 1971). The handiest way to discover what the significant textual variations in a passage are and the arguments for their relative assessment.

Burton H. Throckmorton, Jr., *Gospel Parallels* (New York: Thomas Nelson & Sons, 1949, 1957). The RSV text of the synoptic gospels set in parallel columns so that variations between the three accounts are easily noted.

Kurt Aland, *Synopsis of the Four Gospels* (London/ New York: United Bible Societies, 1972). RSV and Greek, with John added to the Synoptics.

G. Kittel and G. Friedrich, eds., *Theological Dictionary of the New Testament*, trans. G.W. Bromiley (Grand Rapids: Eerdmans, 1964-74, 9 vols.). A massive study of the theological vocabulary of the Greek New Testament. Excellent for its time, it is now probably too dated, technical, and expensive for regular use by most preachers.

Alan Richardson, ed., *A Theological Word Book of the Bible* (New York: Macmillan, 1951). A handy but aging one-volume listing of the theologically significant words in the New Testament.

Rudolf Bultmann, *The Theology of the New Testament* (New York: Scribner's, 1951-55, 2 vols.). Still the basic introduction even though its treatment of the synoptic gospels is obsolete.

George Buttrick *et al.*, eds., *Interpreter's Dictionary of the Bible* (Nashville: Abingdon, 1962-76, 4 vols. + supplement). An incredibly rich treasure-trove of information.

John L. McKenzie, *Dictionary of the Bible* (Milwaukee: Bruce, 1965). An incredible solo performance by one of the most distinguished Catholic Scripture scholars in America.

Charles M. Laymon, ed., *Interpreter's One-Volume Commentary on the Bible* (Nashville: Abingdon, 1971). An excellent ecumenical effort.

Raymond Brown, Joseph Fitzmyer, and Roland Murphy, *The Jerome Biblical Commentary* (Englewood Cliffs, N.J.: Prentice-Hall, 1968). As good as the names of its editors lead you to expect.

Redaction Criticism

MATTHEW

Gunther Bornkamm, Gerhard Barth, and Heinz Joachim Held, *Tradition and Interpretation in Matthew* (Philadelphia: Westminster, 1963). Pioneer studies by a distinguished German scholar and two of his students.

Jack Dean Kingsbury, *Matthew: Structure, Christology, Kingdom* (Philadelphia: Fortress, 1975). To me, the most convincing study of key theological concepts in Matthew.

MARK

D.E. Nineham, *The Gospel of St. Mark*, "The Pelican Gospel Commentaries" (New York: Seabury Press, 1968). An excellent commentary written at quite a popular level.

Eduard Schweizer, *The Good News According to Mark*, (Richmond: John Knox, 1970). Fine technical scholarship with quite good summaries of the affirmations made in the various pericopes.

Werner Kelber, *Mark's Story of Jesus* (Philadelphia: Fortress Press, 1979). An effort to interpret the storyline of Mark according to the latest scholarly understanding, but with a complete lack of explicit technical reference. A milestone in the effort to make the fruits of scholarship available to a wider public.

LUKE

O.C. Edwards, Jr., *Luke's Story of Jesus* (Philadelphia: Fortress Press, 1981). Written to be a companion to the Kelber volume on Mark. Others are scheduled on Matthew and John.

John Drury, *Luke: A Commentary on the New Testament in Modern English* (New York: Macmillan, 1973). While written for a popular audience, this commentary shows more insight into the points being made by Luke than many commentaries with much more display of technical scholarship.

Luke T. Johnson, *The Literary Function of Possessions in Luke-Acts* (Missoula: Scholars Press, 1977). A doctoral dissertation that deals with an important theological theme in Luke.

David Tiede, *Prophecy and History in Luke-Acts* (Philadelphia: Fortress Press, 1980). A perceptive study of a major motif in Luke's theology.

Only the first volume of Joseph Fitzmyer's "Anchor Bible" Commentary on Luke has appeared so far and I have not yet had opportunity to read it, but I expect it to be excellent.

JOHN

Raymond Brown, *The Gospel According to John*, "The Anchor Bible" (Garden City, N.Y.: Doubleday, 1966-70, 2 vols.) Magisterial.

_____, *The Community of the Beloved Disciple* (New York: Paulist Press, 1979). An updating of Brown's theory on the various stages of editing in the Johannine corpus and their relation to the history of the Johannine community.

THE Q DOCUMENT

Richard Edwards, *A Theology of Q* (Philadelphia: Fortress Press, 1976). The best study available of the theology that lies behind the material common to Matthew and Luke and of the community that produced it.

Other Biblical Studies

Joachim Jeremias, *The Parables of Jesus* (New York: Scribner's, 1954). Indispensable for preaching.

Eta Linnemann, *Jesus of the Parables* (New York: Harper & Row, 1966). Exciting study of the way that Jesus' parables function as arguments.

Walter Wink, *The Bible in Human Transformation: Toward a New Paradigm for Biblical Study* (Philadelphia: Fortress Press, 1973). This work proposes a form of group meditation on the Bible that makes it relevant to life today.

Richmond Lattimore, *The Four Gospels and the Revelation* (New York: Farrar Straus Giroux, 1979). This translation is the most literal (and thus nearest to the original Greek) that I know.

English Composition

William Strunk, Jr. and E.B. White, *The Elements of Style*, 3rd ed., (New York: Macmillan, 1979). The best friend that anyone who wanted to write clear English sentences ever had.

Robert Graves and Alan Hodge, *The Reader Over Your Shoulder* (New York: Vintage Books, 1979). The would-be writer's second best friend.

Oxford American Dictionary (New York: Avon, 1980). Finally a dictionary that dares to prescribe usage.

Miscellaneous

Peter Berger, *Facing Up to Modernity: Excursions in Society, Politics, and Religion* (New York: Basic Books, 1977). While I have profited enormously from many of the books of this great sociologist of knowledge, the two references in this book to him are to essays in this book.

Urban T. Holmes, *Turning to Christ: A Theology of Renewal and Evangelization* (New York: Seabury Press, 1981). Probably the masterpiece of this prematurely deceased Anglican theologian.

Acknowledgments

Abingdon Press, for William Skudlarek OSB, *The Word in Worship: Preaching in a Liturgical Context*; and for Myron R. Chartier, *Preaching as Communication: An Interpersonal Perspective*.

The America Press, for Walter M. Abbot (general editor) and Joseph Gallagher (translation editor), *The Documents of Vatican II*, copyright © 1966 by The America Press. Used by permission of The America Press.

Baker Book House, for Halford E. Luccock, *In the Minister's Workshop*, copyright ©1944 by Whitmore & Stone, reprinted 1977 by Baker Book House and used by permission.

Fortress Press, for H. Grady Davis, *Design for Preaching*, copyright © 1958 by Fortress Press; and for Edmund A. Steimle, Morris J. Niedenthal, and Charles L. Rice, *Preaching the Story*, copyright © 1980 by Fortress Press. Used by permission of Fortress Press.

Bill Granger, for an excerpt from his column in the *Chicago Tribune*, April 6, 1982.

Harcourt, Brace, Jovanovich, for T.S. Eliot," Choruses from 'The Rock,'" as in *The Complete Poems and Plays, 1909–50*.